ENCYCLOPAEDIA OF EMINENT THINKERS

VOLUME-IV: **RADHA KRISHNAN**

Encyclopaedia of Eminent Thinkers Series

Vol. I. The Political Thought of **Mahatma Gandhi**
Vol. II. The Political Thought of **Nehru**
Vol. III. The Political Thought of **Rabindra Nath Tagore**
Vol. IV. The Political Thought of **Radhakrishnan**
Vol. V. The Political Thought of **Vinoba**
Vol. VI. The Political Thought of **Aurobindo**
Vol. VII. The Political Thought of **Jayaprakash Narayan**
Vol. VIII. The Political Thought of **Vivekananda**
Vol. IX. The Political Thought of **Ambedkar**
Vol. X. The Political Thought of **M.N. Roy**

About the Author

K.S. Bharathi did his Master's Degree in Gandhian Thought, Peace-Science, Economics, and Political Science. He also did Postgraduate Diplomas in Politics, Public Administration, Population Dynamics, Gandhian Thought, Tourism, and Telgu. He has contributed some articles in learned journals. He is the author of : *Foundation of Gandhian Thought, Gandhi and Humanity, Socio-Religious Thoughts of Mahatma Gandhi, The Philosophy of Sarvodya, The Satyagraha of Mahatma Gandhi, Gandhi and Nehru, Foundations of Ambedkar Thought, The Social Philosophy of Mahatma Gandhi, Gandhian Approach to Rural Development, The Relevance of Gandhi, Gandhi and Vinoba, The Philosophical Foundations of Gandhian Thought, The Political Thought of Gandhi, The Economic Thought of Gandhi, The Social Thought of Gandhi*, and *The Quintessence and Chronology of Gandhi*. At present, he is the Head of the Postgraduate Department of Gandhian Thought of Nagpur University. He is the Chairman of the Board of Studies of Gandhian Thought, member of the Academic Council, member of the Faculty of Social Sciences, member of the Board of Examination, and member of the Doctoral Research Committee of Nagpur University.

ENCYCLOPAEDIA OF EMINENT THINKERS

VOLUME FOUR

THE POLITICAL THOUGHT OF RADHAKRISHNAN

K.S. BHARATHI
Head, P.G. Department of Gandhian Thought
Nagpur University, Nagpur

CONCEPT PUBLISHING COMPANY, NEW DELHI-110 059

ISBN 81-7022-688-0 (Vol. 4)

ISBN 81-7022-684-8 (Series)

First Published 1998

Published and Printed by
Ashok Kumar Mittal
Concept Publishing Company
A/15-16, Commercial Block, Mohan Garden,
NEW DELHI-110059 (India)

Ph 5648039, 5649024
Fax 091-11-5648068

TO
BHAVANI

PREFACE

The relation between politics and religion was not primarily in institutions and movements for social change, but centred largely in the inner spiritual regeneration of the individual resulting in compassionate action in society. It would appear that, according to Radhakrishnan, spiritually insightful individuals would be the main transforming agents in society. Modern Man without losing his social consciousness or conscience, must rediscover within himself a source of individual initiative sufficiently strong to cope with social despotisms. Religion is a dynamic process.

Mankind is a unit for Radhakrishnan, but religion itself is a primarily individual concern. This is partly an idea taken over from Western liberalism and often repeated today by members of our own secular elite. They say that politics is public while religion is private. For Radhakrishnan this Western liberal idea is confirmed by the Hindu tradition as it has developed.

The life and work of Radhakrishnan has been discussed in the first chapter. His views on Education has been covered in the second chapter. His views on Religion and Philosophy, Hindu *Dharma*-I, Hindu *Dharma*-II have been analysed in the next three chapters. His views on Politics has been discussed in the last chapter. Radhakrishnan's original writings on Hindu *Dharma* have been reproduced in fourth and fifth chapters.

I would like to place on record my indebtedness to scholars and thinkers whose ideas enabled me to bring out this book. I gratefully acknowledge the scholars from whose works I have drawn citations viz. Dr. G. Parthasarathi, Dr. S. Gopal, Dr. S. Radhakrishnan, Dr. Clarissa Rodrigues, Dr. Glyn Richards, and Dr. J.J. Lipner.

So far as the writing of this book is concerned, whatever success I have achieved is due to relentless efforts and encouragement of Dr. P.S.G. Kumar, Head, Department of Library and Information Science, Nagpur University. I sincerely express my gratitude to him.

I express my warm thanks to Mr. P.N. Hardas, and Mr. S.T. Patale of Nagpur University.

I am indebted to Concept Publishing Company, New Delhi for publishing this book in such a short span of time. Finally I hold myself to blame for the errors and shortcomings, if any. This work would not have been completed without the grace of Lord Venkateswara of Tirumala and Alamelu Thayar of Tiruchanur.

K.S. BHARATHI

CONTENTS

1

LIFE AND WORKS OF RADHAKRISHNAN

Radhakrishnan was a multi-faceted personality. He was a diamond with many splendoured radiance, a flash of light, sometimes blindingly brilliant. He belongs to the galaxy of outstanding leaders and philosophers produced by the Indian National Movement. He died at the age of 87, after spending more than a half of his life in colonial India. He was an associate of Gandhiji and Nehru but unlike them both he was neither a tribune nor a political leader. As a young man, he was involved in research and pedagogical activities, and was known as an expert on Indian culture and philosophy, a talented teacher and lecturer, and an original thinker who developed his own philosophical system.

Radhakrishnan was born on 5 September 1888 at Tirutani in Madras city. He was the second son of his parents, Sarvapalli Veeraswami and Sitamma. In the middle of eighteenth century, Veeraswami's ancestors had moved from the village of Sarvapalli but retained the word Sarvapalli in their names to indicate their place of origin. He joined the primary Board High School at Tirutani and spent about four years learning arithmetic, geography, Indian history, Telugu and elementary English. In 1896, he was shifted to the Hermansburg Evangelical Luthern Mission School at Tirupati. He was clever enough to win scholarships but was by no means studious; nor was he interested in games. His main activity was to play truant and walk long distances from village to village, using the scholarship money and whatever was sent from home to pay for his food *en route*. He passed the matriculation examination of the University of Madras and won a scholarship to Voorhee's College. He was more influenced by Swami Vivekananda.

In May 1903, at the age of sixteen, Radhakrishnan was married to Sivakamu, aged ten. Her father, a railway station-master, had died in her infancy, and her mother was in no position to seek or buy for her a young man who was heir to property or of established ability. Radhakrishnan got the first daughter in 1908 and then during the next fifteen years, he had six more children. In the early years of their marriage, he and Sivakamu found it mutually satisfying and infused with all the warmth and humour of intimate companionship. He always regarded himself as happily married. In 1904, he passed the first arts examination in the first class and won a scholarship to the Christian College at Madras for the BA courses.

Radhakrishnan had no deep sense of vocation for philosophy. His choice of subject was more by accident than by design; and time and again during his life, he tried to get away from the main pursuit of philosophy only to be foiled by circumstances. The Christian College had at this time a high reputation. Of the teachers of philosophy, he was touched by the kindness of William Skinner. In 1906, he obtained the B.A. degree with first class honours and was the best student of that year in philosophy. He thought of switching to the law but this assumed financial resources which he did not possess. Then he joined M.A. classes in philosophy. In partial fulfilment of the requirements of the M.A. degree, he submitted a dissertation titled *The Ethics of the Vedanta and Its Metaphysical Presuppositions*. The thesis was published in a limited edition by a local press and is now a collector's piece. He accepted the Christian criticisms of Hindu practices and social institutions.

Radhakrishnan outlines the history of Indian philosophy which to him culminates in the philosophy of *Samkara*: 'The grandeur of spiritual oneness which very few thinkers can appreciate is brought out most sublimely'. *Samkara*'s system is to him a combination of religion, metaphysics and ethics; and Radhakrishnan contends that, contrary to general assumption, in this philosophy are found the elements of an ethical science though not a perfected system of ethics. When he had got his M.A. degree in January 1909, it was suggested to him that he apply for one of the scholarships offered every year by the Government of India for Indian students to study at Oxford or Cambridge. He needed employment desperately and tried for various jobs in Madras without success. He was appointed to a substantive post of sub-assistant inspector of schools in an area far from the city but directed to fill a temporary vacancy as Malayalam Master in the Presidency College at Madras. A few months later, he was deputed to the teacher's training college at Saidapet to obtain a diploma in teaching.

To earn extra money Radhakrishnan apart from continuing tuition, took on as many examinerships as he could get. Financial necessity was also responsible for the writing of his next book. In 1912, he brought out a small book titled *Essentials of Psychology* and sold all his rights in the book for the lump sum of Rs 500. This book indicates the strength of Radhakrishnan as a teacher. He was always a very clear expositor of even the most abstruse topic. This ability he manifested from the start of his career. In 1911, he returned to the Presidency College and served there for the next five years, first as additional assistant professor and then from 1914, an assistant professor of philosophy. His influence with his students was not based only on his mastery of the material and facility of expression.

In his student days at Madras Radhakrishnan made no great friendships. He was generally known as a promising scholar. At Saidapet, he met T.K. Doraiswami, a fellow-trainee and specialist in economics; and from then till his death in 1961 Doraiswami was devoted to him. Doraiswami did not claim to be his intellectual equal but looked after his finances in these early years when he had to worry about them. From 1916, when he was posted outside Madras, M.A. Candeth and he maintained a steady correspondence, and Candeth, a prolific letter-writer, kept him abreast of official and other gossip. His years in Christian institutions had given him a firm grounding in the *Bible,* European thought and English literature; and on these he never ceased to build. He set himself, during his years at Presidency College to learn Sanskrit with the help of *pandits* and then studied the classics, the *Upanishads* and the *Gita*, and the commentaries on them.

With a vague but powerful ambition to secure recognition for the validity of the intrinsic elements of Hindu thought in the world outside, Radhakrishnan was keen to publish his articles in the philosophical journals of the West. In 1911 the *International Journal of Ethics* published an article by him called 'The Ethics of the *Bhagavad Gita* and Kant'. The same journal also published, three years later, two articles on aspects of the *Vedanta.* While the teachings of Hinduism seemed to him basically sound, he blamed its current practices for India's political weakness and abject condition. He paid tribute to Gandhi's work in South Africa; but when he met Gandhi in Madras at this time, the interview was not a success.

Radhakrishnan's explanation of Tagore's eminence brings to mind the belief of Coleridge that no man was ever a great poet without being at the same time a profound philosopher ; for to Radhakrishnan Tagore's work was the outcome and expression of the Indian ideals of philosophy, religion and art. He contended that the true Hindu outlook demands that finite man should strive for the infinite and seek to reconcile the self and the not-self. He always attached importance to suffering as the way of salvation, the chance offered by God to draw man to his real destiny. This was to him the message of Hinduism and of Christianity as well.

Elsewhere in the book, however, Radhakrishnan shifted the emphasis from confrontation to each civilisation absorbing the best of the other, and pleaded more for the assimilative synthesis which he thought had always bleen the characteristic of India—the integration of the old and the new, of the East and the West. He regarded caste as a system not without rationale and indeed inspired by a right hierarchy of values, as against Western society motivated by economic principles and structured on class; but life had departed from the caste system and it needed drastic overhaul. Though the book came out at the time of the armistice in November 1918, it was widely noticed. The reviews were as expected. His clear, epigrammatic style was generally commended, though one critic charged him with occasional word-spinning and elaboration of the obvious. His account of Christianity and refusal to accept major Christian influence on Tagore naturally did not secure unqualified approval.

Radhakrishnan was happy with his work in the Presidency College and turned down the offer of a more lucrative post at Pachaiyappa's College, a private institution in the Madras city. In 1916, he was transferred to Ananthapur as a junior lecturer, but this exile lasted only for three months and he returned to Presidency College in September 1916 as Professor of Philosophy. He expected to hold that post for the next thirty years. But, in 1917 he was transferred from the Presidency College to the College of Rajahmundry to make way for a non-Brahmin, accepted by all as less able but senior to him in the service. To him, this was, a disappointment. He was unhappy out of Madras and, seeing no chance of getting back soon to the Presidency College began seriously to consider moving to the newly founded university in the state of Mysore. He moved from Rajahmundry to Mysore as additional professor of philosophy in July 1918. The appointment was for five years on a fixed monthly salary of Rs 500.

In a sense, Radhakrishnan was an absolute idealist in the Western tradition before he became a sympathetic exponent of the *Vedanta*. Philosophy to him was an intellectual attempt to organise the whole of experience, and religion must not influence philosophy but be justified by it. Even religious feeling must pass through the fire of metaphysical thinking. Religion is not the starting point but the terminus of philosophy. True philosophy would result in true religion and to him, this was the *Advaita Vedanta.* This was the only philosophical religion which could be justified by logical seriousness and not just by soft thinking, emotional fervour or moral earnestness.

In 1920, the Reign received considerable attention. Christian theologians were concerned by his implicit attack on Christianity. In philosophical circles the book was more favourably considered and was prescribed for study in a number of British and American universities as providing a clear and able exposition and discussion of the fundamentals of contemporary philosophy. Hinman's main criticism of the book was that the elements of a speculative theism which were inevitably involved in Radhakrishnan's position were not developed but rather quietly suppressed. The other element in this book which draws away from Radhakrishnan's vigorous defence of reason and logic is his unqualified appreciation of what he describes as true mysticism as against magic and occultism.

Radhakrishnan planned a series of novels depicting the changing India, of how, in his view, the people should react to the contact with Western ideas and absorb these into Indian tradition. The blend of the new with the old should result in securing the best of both worlds. The title page of *The Crime of Leela* designates it as the first of the stories of Indian life in transition. His experience of the world was still limited, and wide reading is no substitute. He could not in this novel move out of academic elitism. All the characters are bloodless and one-dimensional. His views on women as delineated in this novel also remained basically unaltered. He recognised that women were the equals of men and there was no justification for sexual discrimination.

An air of general friendliness and a new interest in women did not encompass the whole of Radhakrishnan's social efforts in Mysore. His main constituency was the students. His lectures, clear and lightened with touches of humour, drew many from other departments. But a teacher's reputation depends on much more than teaching alone. Radhakrishnan commanded attention and affection by the atmosphere created by his personality. His powerful memory enabled him to recognise each one of his students and he was natural with them, treating them with an unaffected familiarity and concerning himself with their problems. He was confident that his work, born of faith in himself and inspired by the pride of patriotism had its own contribution to make to the national effort.

Radhakrishnan was aware that the Government of Mysore were not appreciative of his work. So, when in 1920, the post of professor of philosophy in the Presidency College was allotted to the Indian Educational Service, he let the Government of Madras know that if promoted from the provincial service and offered that professorship, he was prepared to return from Mysore. But the British officials in the department of education were still unwilling to set aside the claims of the person who had displaced Radhakrishnan in the Presidency College in 1917. In 1920, with his appointment to the George V chair and the decision to promote him to the Indian Educational Service, Radhakrishnan had at last, from the viewpoint of his professional carrier, arrived. The struggle for acceptance was finally over. The George V professorship was the most prestigious chair in philosophy in India and doubled his salary from Rs 500 to Rs 1,000 a month. He felt slightly uneasy at the thought of shifting to Calcutta. In the last week of February 1921 he handed over charge.[1]

To introduce Radhakrishnan to Calcutta, Sir Ashutosh Mukherjee arranged for him to deliver a public lecture on a philosophical topic. The large Senate Hall was crowded and Radhakrishnan made the expected impact with his wide range and quick fluency. Radhakrishnan's only friend at this time was the physicist C.V. Raman, also still not fully at home in Calcutta and a fellow-victim of such resentment as there was of non-Bengalis. Indian Philosophy was a massive work in two volumes, the first published in 1923 and the second in 1927. He was an astute man of business and, clear-headed about the printing and sales of his own works, gave opinions on the commercial aspects of the writings of other persons which proved so extraordinarily exact. He did not call his work a history of Indian philosophy, not so much because Dasgupta was at this time bringing out a series of volumes with that title as because he regarded his own effort as an interpretative survey rather than a chronicle.

Though Radhakrishnan disclaimed being a historian this was intellectual history of a high quality : the re-enactment of past thought in the historian's mind, his forming a judgement of its value in the context of his own knowledge. In studying the philosophical thought of the past Radhakrishnan regarded as senseless the idea of an uninterpreted text. He compared the teachings of the Buddha and of Bergson, explained Hinayana Buddhism. Some readers felt that Radhakrishnan tended to lay too much emphasis on the similarities between Indian and Western thought and, in his desire to find parallels, pressed too much meaning out of the original texts.

The critical comments in the West were that Radhakrishnan had too facile a pen and the book suffered from verboseness; a good editor could easily have reduced the length of the two volumes taken together by about a third without diminishing its impact. But the major criticism was that in his effort to combat the general Christian attitude—that philosophy in India was a crass compilation of the crude and the fatuous—Radhakrishnan tended to be aggressive in defence. He had a forward-looking faith in the power of Indian thinkers to renew the spirit of truth by discarding old forms if given the right conditions. Nearly sixty years after publication, the two volumes of *Indian Philosophy*, despite the outdated political rhetoric and, at places, the weakness of being wordy and repetitive, have not been displaced.

When Radhakrishnan joined Calcutta University in March 1921 the students were on strike in obedience to Gandhi's call; and Sir Ashutosh Mukherjee was having problems with the Government of Bengal. On both counts Radhakrishnan's sympathy was naturally against the authorities; but he did not whack the nationalist drum. It seemed to Radhakrishnan a mental derangement on the part of Indians to believe that Gandhi was an authority in economics and education and social reform and everything else merely because he happened to be a spiritual saint. The swing in Radhakrishnan's attitude to Gandhi came early the next year, when Gandhi called off the campaign of civil disobedience because of the burning of a few policemen by a riotous mob and, arrested soon after, made a moving statement in court. Radhakrishnan was now convinced that the movement which Gandhi had initiated was deeply spiritual; non-cooperation was a war of principle waged with the strength of spirit.

Educated throughout in Christian institutions, thought by redoubtable Christian theologians and influenced by their personalities, steeped in the *Bible* and familiar with the writings of Christian thinkers, Radhakrishnan had reacted defensively to the criticisms and disparagement of Hinduism so common in the early years of this century and to the argument that there was no hope for India unless it accepted Christianity. He had then gradually moved on to the offensive. He later suggested that Christianity properly understood had much in common with the fundamentals of Hindu thought.

Radhakrishnan pleaded that Christians, particularly in India, should not stress the aspects of Christian dogma which spoke of the special character of Jesus, of grace to the elect and of eternal torment of the rest, but emphasise those elements which were common to all the great religions. Christianity should help Hinduism to enrich its spirit not by giving of itself but by helping Hinduism to discover what lay in it undeveloped. Hinduism was attempting to slough off its superstitions and purify itself and there was no greater mission for Christians than to help in this process. If the best features of Hinduism and Christianity were brought together, it was not India alone that would be the gainer by this 'Hindu Christianity'.[2]

In 1926 Calcutta University nominated Radhakrishnan as its representative at the Congress of Universities of the British Empire which was to meet in London. Radhakrishnan was not eager to go out of India, and arrival in London at the height of the general strike was not the best introduction to England. To assert that Hinduism was more a way of life than a form of thought, to insist that it was not a static but a resilient religion; a movement, not a position; a process, not a result; a growing tradition, not a fixed revelation, meant that Radhakrishnan had to concern himself with Hindu organisation and behaviour as well as with its theoretical attractiveness. In his lectures on the same subject in the United States Radhakrishnan drew a comparison more familiar to his audiences, and broadly compared the caste system in India with the monopolies in types of jobs which had developed in the United States. The religion expounded by Radhakrishnan may be said to have illustrated the principles of Manchester College on a scale of which those acquainted only with Western religion have no knowledge. The time when he delivered these lectures was obviously one when in India religion and politics could not be kept apart. He was a sensitive patriot and his work was intended as much to assert the primacy of India in matters of faith and spirit as to delineate the main principles of Hinduism.

Radhakrishnan acknowledged that Hindus had carefully protected superstitious rites and customs, and that the doctrine of *karma* was frequently confused with a fatalist outlook. By softening the harsh outlines of traditional Hindu thought and practice he was making it easier for civilised persons to hold to the Hindu faith and to resist the attractions of Christianity. In later years, he himself moved away to positions which were explicitly more qualified. The caste system had changed its character in the process of history and could no longer be regarded as anything more than an insistence on a variety of ways in which the social purpose should be carried out.

Radhakrishnan spoke at the Moral Sciences Club in Cambridge on Bradley and Samkara, and gave three lectures in London on the philosophic basis of Hinduism. From Britain he moved on to the United States. The highlight of his visit to the United States was his performance at the International Congress of Philosophy at Harvard. He gave much thought to his addresses but disliked reading from a written script. At Harvard he was asked to speak at an open session, along with Etienne Gilson, Dewey and Croce, on the role of philosophy in the history of civilisation. This short address, serious in substance, delivered without notes and without hesitation, full of striking phrases and punctuated with humour, carried the audience. Reports of his activities in the West preceded his return and ensured welcome receptions at Bombay, Madras and Calcutta. He criticised the educational policy of the government for not generating in students a sense of national pride and self-respect.

In November 1926 Radhakrishnan returned to Calcutta. This time Jadunath Sarkar was the Vice-Chancellor of Calcutta University. The professors of the university disliked the choice of Sarkar. In his first major address in India on education Radhakrishnan laid down principles which he consistently sponsored for the next four decades. At the outset he denounced a policy which trained students to serve as efficient and docile tools of an external authority but did not help them to become self-respecting citizens of a free nation. University education in India discouraged free mental life and intellectual adventure. Remodelling was essential from the school level upwards, and he favoured guidance of secondary education also by the university, which itself should be dominated by professors and teachers. He suggested adequate salaries and reasonable security of tenure for university and college teachers.

Radhakrishnan was unanimously elected by the concerned faculties as President of the Post-graduate Council of Arts. He found deeply involved in all the clashes that followed in the senate and other university bodies, and was regarded as the leading champion of the teachers and students of Calcutta University against all who sought to encroach on their interests. The differences between Sarkar and the staff and students expanded. To deal with the demonstrations against the Simon Commission on its arrival in Calcutta in February 1928, the Vice-Chancellor sought the support of the police, who beat up the protesting students. Radhakrishnan was appointed by the syndicate to conduct an enquiry, and he reported that the attack on the students was unprovoked and unjustified.[3]

In 1928, at the request of Bishop David of Liverpool, Radhakrishnan wrote a small pamphlet, *The Religion We Need, God and the Modern World* published by Ernest Benn. The purpose of this series was to encourage open discussion of religious problems in order to help Christians make better sense of the world. He was invited to write on the future of civilisation and he dashed it off during a fortnight's vacation in Darjeeling in the summer of 1928. The main purpose of the trip was to lobby with the Bengal government for the selection of the next Vice-Chancellor from among the members of the Mukherjee group. In Kalki, he expanded his address at the International Congress of Philosophy two years earlier. He also, at this time, wrote a long article on Indian philosophy for the new edition of the *Encyclopaedia Britannica.* The decision to have for the first time a separate section on this topic was in itself, in a way, recognition of his work. When he attended the Congress Session in Calcutta as a visitor, approaches were made to him by various members to speak for or against resolutions.

In 1928 L.P. Jacks offered Radhakrishnan the lecturership at Manchester College in comparative religion, held till then by Estlin Carpenter, on a permanent basis or for five years. He declined, for this would have meant leaving Calcutta University, but agreed to take the post for a year, starting from January 1929. He postponed his departure till September and spent the academic year 1929-30 at Oxford. He also agreed to deliver, during that year, the Hibbert Lectures at the universities of Manchester and London. This gave him the opportunity to construct his own metaphysical system. His aim was to show that the universe had value, a meaning and a purpose, and that humanity needed a religion which provided a vital contact with reality, measured up to rigorous metaphysical requirements, satisfied the scientific approach and met the spiritual demands of the time.

In *The Reign* Radhakrishnan had written of reason—Philosophers and faith-philosophers. In 1918 he was in the first category; by 1929 he had moved to the second. Of all his philosophical writings, *An Idealist View* was his most personal utterance. It followed that while in *The Reign* he had criticised religion for distorting philosophy, he now gave a lower role to philosophy. It was to him at this time interpretative rather than creative, not so much an intellectual reconstruction as an exhibition of insights. He contended that all creative work in science, philosophy and art was inspired by intuitive experience. He regarded the literature of his time as essentially trivial. Even the greatest masters, Shaw, Wells and Bridges, did not seem to him to touch the heights of genius. To him, intuitive insight was essential also for the highest races of ethical life.

Although in 1926 Radhakrishnan had repeatedly advocated the honest acceptance of lack of understanding, and even in 1928 conceded that the relation between the universal spirit and the cosmic process was enveloped in impenetrable mystery, obviously this problem continued to nag him and in 1929 he came up with a possible answer. God is organic with the world. Life beyond time may take us to the Absolute, but God is essentially bound up with the life in time. When *An Idealist View of Life* was published in 1932, the book secured greater attention than the lectures had done. Though the critics were not converted, *An Idealist View* was the most distinguished of his writings and his major claim on posterity. He drew a complete map of current knowledge, used it in a fresh way to support his arguments and rounded it off with an original hypothesis. Above all, he spoke from the depths and clearly with the intuitive insight which was to him basic.[4]

As for his emphasis on intuition, Radhakrishnan always contended that he was not an anti-intellectual, providing rational justification for a basically anti-rational attitude. His ideas were based on the notion in the *Upanishads* of the comradeship of scientific knowledge and intuitive experience. In his later writings he emphasised that the human mind does not function in fractions. He felt no need in later years, in the light of new knowledge and experience, to revise the essentials of his philosophical system. During this year at Oxford he had much else to do besides delivering the Hibberts Lectures. In his courses on comparative religion at Manchester College he gave the discipline a new slant.

Radhakrishnan was particularly critical of missionaries in India and did not hesitate to describe the Anglian church as linked up with British imperialism. The study of other religions, indispensable for the proper understanding of one's own, had to be based on the assumption that one religion was as good as another and none was final or perfect. He agreed to requests to speak in various parts of Britain, and, towards the end of his stay in the spring and summer of 1930, he was giving a major address almost every day. The political situation in India was by now heading to a crisis. The Congress party had declared its objective to be complete independence and Gandhi was preparing for a campaign of civil disobedience. With so many demands, entailing much hard work and constant travelling, he was by the end longing to be back at rest in his little corner in Calcutta.

Within a few weeks of Radhakrishnan's arrival in Calcutta, there were regular attacks on his writings. The issue of the *Modern Review* for January 1929 carried a long letter from Sinha charging him with plagiarism and citing passages from the thesis and his book. A systematic effort was being made by dedicated detractors to destroy his reputation as a scholar and public figure. So, he had no option but, in the summer of 1929, to file, in the Calcutta High Court, a plaint for defamation against Sinha and Ramananda Chatterjee, and seek Rs 100,000 as damages. Sinha promptly lodged a counter-claim of Rs 20,000 for literary piracy. The cases were finally taken up four years later, in the spring of 1933. Ganganatha Jha and Kuppuswami Sastri voluntarily came to Calcutta to give evidence in support of Radhakrishnan. In April 1933 both the plaints, about defamation and piracy, were simultaneously withdrawn.

In 1925, when the establishment of a university in the Andhra area was in the air, Radhakrishnan toyed with the idea of returning from Calcutta as its first professor of philosophy, but nothing came of this. In December 1927, at the invitation of the Vice-Chancellor, C.R. Reddy, he delivered the address at the first convocation of the new university. He stressed that merit should be the sole criterion in the choice of professors, for only they—if they had a zeal for research which would create a zest in teaching—could develop the atmosphere of scientific habit which imparted value to university training. In 1928, he received from the Andhra University his first-honorary degree. On this visit to the Andhra areas he was involved in more than academic activity. He presided over the Andhra students' conference at Guntur and the session of the Andhra Mahasabha at Nandyal.

Reddy resigned in December and the election took place in March 1931, ironically the day after Gandhi and the Viceroy reached a settlement. Radhakrishnan was deeply involved in negotiations with the Bengal government on the future of the postgraduate departments, for the official grants earmarked for this purpose had lapsed in 1930. But, urged by his supporters in Waltair not to let them down, he took up the Andhra Vice-Chancellorship in May 1931. He made it clear that appointments should be made on purely academic grounds and all academic and administrative questions should be left to the university. The list of recruits to the faculty of the Andhra University in the thirties is a roll-call of distinguished Indians in the sixties and seventies. Humayun Kabir and Hiren Mukherjee were among the first to be chosen. C.V. Raman was co-opted as a member of the syndicate, took charge of the drafting of the syllabuses in science and was appointed honorary professor of physics.

Radhakrishnan within two years made the Andhra University, located in a remote place, one of the most exciting academic centres in India. He acquired for the university about fifty-four acres in the upland areas. By 1934 the two Colleges and one hostel had been completed; two more hostels were ready the next year and, by the time of his departure in 1936, the construction of the library and the clock tower had been completed. He also secured in 1935 sanction for the payment of advance increments in recognition of research of quality. He attached every student in the university colleges to a tutor to exercise general supervision. To the library he gave special attention. He drew up a list of the journals in the humanities and the social sciences to which the university should subscribe and asked Raman to assume responsibility for scientific periodicals. Members of the staff were encouraged to give extension lectures in Waltair as well as in other Andhra towns. On 19 May, 1936, the day before he handed over charge, the Government of Madras wrote to the Medical Council recommending recognition of medical degrees conferred by the Andhra University. So all but the last formal step had been taken.[5]

In his five years at Waltair, Radhakrishnan laid the foundations in every sense of the Andhra University. His administrative and organisational talents, working on the basis that only the best will do, were seen at their best. His assessment of academic worth was sounder than his judgement of human character in general. Elected Vice-Chancellor in 1931 for three years, he was unanimously re-elected in 1934. This would have taken him on till February 1937, and Waltair, half-way between Madras and Calcutta, was a pleasant place to live in. He resided in a large house near the beach and had time to spend with his growing children. In February 1936, he informed the senate of the Andhra University that he would lay down office in May and steps should be taken to elect his successor.

Radhakrishnan welcomed the fact that the students were not free from the blessed contagion of unrest, and asked them to live a dedicated life with no thought of personal comfort. His reputation as scholar and speaker led to requests from various universities for the delivery of convocation addresses, and he accepted most of these invitations, for he thought it of importance to communicate with educated young men and women. Irwin, rare among viceroys for his interest in matters of the mind and spirit, decided also that Radhakrishnan's stature as a philosopher merited official recognition. He paid his homage of love to Gandhi for his example of self-respect and moral courage. The attachment to Gandhi, now embarked on a campaign to improve the lot of the untouchables in Hindu society, grew stronger.

The International Committee for Intellectual Co-operation, of which Radhakrishnan was a member for eight years from 1931, was for him an ideal forum. In 1935 he persuaded the Inter-University Board of India to function also as a national commission. In him, nationalism and internationalism were never apart. He planned a second series of Hibbert Lectures with an emphasis on the influence of his philosophy of religion on moral life. He also considered writing, as a sequel of *Kalki*, a book on the moral law, entitled *Acceptance and Adventure*. However, he did not get down to writing this book. Rather, his energies were engaged in writing chapters on Hinduism for *The Legacy of India* and for a volume on *Modern India and the West*. He was also busy in editing a collection of *Essays on Contemporary Indian Philosophy*.

In 1936 Radhakrishnan shifted his base to Britain, and there it remained for the next three years. The appointment at Oxford was obviously of more than professional significance. He had never been a secluded philosopher. His patriotism had stood out both in his stress on the vitality of Indian thought and in his non-philosophical addresses. He was a well-known figure, generally respected for his learning and lucid eloquence and liked as a personality.

Radhakrishnan continued to support the leadership of Gandhi and, in addition, felt increasingly in sympathy with Nehru. Fascism, dictatorships, imperialism, aggressive nationalism and the kind of education which prepared youth for war were all intertwined and he, like Nehru, had no doubt that the fundamental conditions of the existing order had to be altered to pave the way for a new society with civil liberties for all individuals and independence for all nations. He was never an advocate of a world religion, or any effort to amalgamate bits and pieces of various beliefs. He favoured a pluralistic world with no universal churches. He believed that the universe had a sovereign purpose and history was a meaningful process.

Radhakrishnan tried to convince the British that Gandhi was their best friend, reported to Zetland, the secretary of state, that he had talked to Gandhi, who was in a receptive mood, and urged the British to settle matters regarding federation with Gandhi while he was still around and in charge. The election of Subhas Chander Bose as President of the Congress should be a warning to them. But he was not optimistic.

He spoke to Gandhi of his intent to edit a collection of essays and reflections on Gandhi's life and work to be presented to him on his seventieth birthday in October 1939. Gandhi gave his permission and Radhakrishnan went ahead. He himself, in a long tradition, developed the deeper thought and meaning of Gandhi's life and work. To him Gandhi was essentially a religious person who had become a political worker because his religious outlook meant a commitment to the whole of humanity.

Eastern Religions and Western Thought, based on his lectures at Oxford and elsewhere, had just been published and received with enthusiasm. He had argued, with style, scholarship and much spiritual feeling, that the problem of contemporary civilisation was to gain a unity of soul; and this challenge could be met if a philosophy could be developed which combined the best of European humanism and Asian religion. He drew attention to the common elements in Christianity and Hinduism and emphasised the points in which they moved in the same direction. He arrived in Durban with a formidable reputation. His addresses on comparative religion at the universities were given to audiences which overflowed into other rooms, while his general talks to Indian societies, African schools and rotary and ladies' clubs drew considerable numbers despite the reluctance of the European press to give publicity to him and his visit. *Indian Opinion,* the journal started by Gandhi and at this time edited by his son, wrote that Radhakrishnan's short visit to South Africa was like a flash of light from heaven.

Radhakrishnan pressed Britain to transfer the substance of self-government immediately and supported the demand of the Congress for a clear statement of Britain's objectives. He suggested that in purely internal matters such as revenue and public health Indians should be allowed to determine the future. He suggested a dyarchic approach, with further consideration after ten years. The new government under Churchill, ignoring offers of cooperation from the Congress, were prepared for no imaginative offer such as Radhakrishnan sought. In his speeches in 1941 he emphasised the shortcomings of a civilisation which had made two World Wars possible and called for the spread of the spiritual outlook for which India had always stood.

The University of Banaras, set up in 1917 as a nursery of Hindu culture, had by 1939 developed into the largest residential university in the country, with advanced courses both in the sciences and in the traditional classics.

Radhakrishnan was unwilling to give up his chair at that university and, at the start, served in Banares as a weekend Vice-Chancellor, travelling up on Friday by the night train and returning to Calcutta on Monday morning. Within two years of Radhakrishnan taking up the Vice-Chancellorship, a quarter of the debt was wiped off; and in addition donations were procured for specific purposes such as buildings and fellowships. Under his firm and continuous guidance the university steadied itself and even gathered momentum. Such a smooth tenure of the Vice-Chancellorship lasted for less than three years. He had made no secret of his sympathy with the Congress and resisted official efforts to control opinion in the university. When the Government of the United Provinces objected to some leaflets distributed among the students, he agreed that the government had a tenable viewpoint.

In 1942 Radakrishnan did what he could to prevent a head-on collision between the government and the Congress. The day the All India Congress Committeee met in Bombay, he appealed to the Viceroy to form a coalition cabinet of the Congress and the Muslim League with the commander-in-chief in sole command of the military movements. As Vice-Chancellor, he sought to dissuade students from indulging in violent activities even while he protected the university from the drastic measures which Hallett's government sought to impose. His support of the Congress and particularly his loyalty to Gandhi, even though he was not a formal member of the party, was a matter of surprise only to the governor. He concluded his Kamala Lectures at Calcutta University in December 1942 with an unqualified tribute to Gandhi. Throughout this long period of crisis his literary work had not suffered, He wrote and delivered the Kamala Lectures at Calcutta on religion and the problems of social reconstruction.

Radhakrishnan's position in these years was very critical of the Muslim League. He considered seriously a plan for training young persons to preach Hinduism at its best and, more explicitly than before, spoke of Hinduism as alone being capable of giving modern civilisation a soul and men and women a principle to live by. In June 1945 he reminded the Viceroy that the British Government, which could not be absolved of responsibility for the communal problem, had therefore an obligation to do their utmost to build a free, united and democratic India. During the Simla Conference, on learning that the Muslim League was being intransigent, he urged the Viceroy not to give in to Jinnah and betray the large number of Muslims outside the League. In the pause that followed the failure of the Simla Conference he gave his attention mostly to the university. The end of the war had brought its own problems.

Radhakrishnan had become more than a figure on the sidelines; and it is not surprising that when, later in the year, the Constituent Assembly came into existence, the senior leaders of the Congress unhesitatingly invited him to be one of the non-Congressmen who would be put by by the party for election to the Assembly. Fiercely critical of the British role in setting Hindus and Muslims against each other, it was inconceivable to him that India should be a dominion. She had no sense of belonging to a commonwealth that supported racist policies in South Africa. The emphasis placed by him on tolerance and patience as constituting the genius of India was generally appreciated as timely.

The academic and other engagements, compelling long absences from India, led Radhakrishnan to take steps to divest himself of the Vice-Chancellorship of Banaras University. When Malaviya died in November 1946 Radhakrishnan felt obliged to stay on a while longer and suggested to Mukherjee that he come as Pro-Vice-Chancellor and look after the day-to-day administration. In addition to his work at Oxford and UNESCO, he had agreed to spend three months in Australia in 1947 as the guest of the Australian National University, and a semester the next year at the University of Southern California. He also set afoot a proposal after August 1947 to convert the Hindu University into a national university. His edition of the *Bhagavad Gita* was published in the spring of 1948.

With the success of the *Bhagavad Gita*, Radhakrishnan settled down to a long-term programme of translating the *Dhammapada*, the Buddhist work, and the other two major works of the Hindu canon, the *Upanishads* and the *Brahma Sutra*. Nehru obviously looked on Radhakrishnan as the most clear-headed authority on education in India. In 1938 he had appointed him chairman of the education sub-committee of the national planning committee. He now consulted him on senior appointments in the ministry of education and, in Augast 1948, asked him to take a year's leave from Oxford to head a commission to study the working of Indian universities in all its aspects with a view to recommending measures for their improvement. The only major and immediate result of the recommendations of the Radhakrishnan Commission was the establishment of the University Grants Commission, with substantial benefits to the autonomy and development of Indian universities.[6]

On 16 April 1949, Nehru requested Radhakrishnan to take up the ambassador post in Moscow. It was obviously the first step in drawing him out of the academic scene and into wider spheres of public activity. To those who regarded his philosophic work as unique and irreplaceable, this could seem a betrayal. The appointment announced in July 1949 was seen as unusual and generally welcomed. He had not visited the Soviet Union earlier. The Soviet authorities were clearly intrigued by him. They did not relish his attachment to Oxford and his continued holding of the chair; but the absence from Moscow for half the year that this entailed they did not resent. While in Moscow, Radhakrishnan, having ensured that his staff was wholly Indian, left the day-to-day work of the embassy to them. He was on cordial terms with his colleagues in the diplomatic corps but was not particularly close to the British or American ambassador, or anyone else.

Radhakrishnan's arrival in Moscow in September 1949 coincided with a new phase in the cold war. He had a personal position in the world and he saw no reason to abandon it merely because he had been persuaded to serve as an ambassador. He lived through a severe winter, with the temperature dropping to thirty five to forty degrees below zero. He never missed his walk round the block both in the morning and in the evening even though his nose was frostbitten, and otherwise carried on with his writing and reading. He found that Stalin in person was less formidable than one's thought of him. His main anxiety was about better relations between the great powers. He had gained the impression, when talking to Stalin, that the Soviet leader was keen on an understanding with the West and was not pessimistic about reaching it. Nehru requested him to stay on for another year, which was likely to be critical from every point of view, even if it meant Radhakrishnan's absence for five months from his post.

On 25 June, 1950 fighting broke out in Korea. The Government of India accepted the two resolutions of the Security Council deeming North Korea an aggressor and asking all members of the United Nations to render assistance to the organisation and to South Korea. Radhakrishnan objected that the resolutions of the Security Council were the decisions of one bloc, for the Soviet Union had been absent and Yugoslavia had voted against; and for India to support these resolutions was to persuade the United States that in a crisis India would be with them. He had expressed his concern about the dangers inherent in the Taiwan situation and urged recognition of People's China as a great and noble act by America as leader of the free world. Departing from Moscow for the winter of 1950, his attention shifted to explaining Soviet policy and motives to the outside world and stressing the danger of war breaking out because the two sides were lacking in communication. He said that the United States should take Russia at her word and press her, for withdrawal of all foreign troops from both West and East Germany.

At the non-official level Radhakrishnan encouraged the Society of Friends in Britain to build contacts in the Soviet Union and helped the Quaker Mission of peace and goodwill on its visit to that country. He went ahead in his given task of explaining India's policy and furtheing good relations with the Soviet Union. In the early months of 1951 the Kashmir issue again came up before the Security Council, and the United States and Britain introduced a resolution which was wholly unacceptable to India. Passing through London he spoke to Zarubin, the Soviet ambassador, and gained the impression that Soviet Russia might Veto the resolution. As his second year in Moscow was drawing to its end, Nehru requested him to continue for another year on the same terms of spending six months at Oxford.

Radhakrishnan had got the impression that there was no problem then dividing the world that could not be settled by discussion and negotiation. Stalin was suspicious of the Western powers but desired peace. Radhakrishnan believed that some progress could be made on the problem of Germany. He had conveyed to the British and American authorities the desire of the Soviet government for peace, just as he had minced no words in telling the rulers at Moscow, from Stalin downwards, the reasons for the deep suspicion in the West of Soviet policies. This was the most important in itself and explains the value of his presence in Moscow.

Radhakrishnan had had some hesitations about accepting the Vice-Presidentship. It did not seem to him worthwhile to give up the chair at Oxford and his work outside India for such a limited role. He frequently asserted that he was no more than a member of the government on the decorative side. His main purpose was to draw attention to what he regarded as the essentials of Indian culture and the need to vivify them in the contemporary context. Even before going to Moscow he had spoken in public about the urgency of major economic and social change and from Russia he continued to press these views on the leaders in Delhi.

Nehru relied on Radhakrishnan's understanding of the times in which they lived and of the broad forces at work, recognised in him a reassuring presence who imparted a touch of highmindedness to the government, and consulted him on big issues as well as small. The relationship, nurtured by affinity of aspiration and trust, gradually spread beyond the region of public affairs. About the necessity of rapid economic and social change, he continued as Vice-President to be as outspoken as ever before. Nehru's utilisation of Radhakrishnan in domestic matters generally was a sounding-board and source of disinterested advice. On education he regarded him as the greatest authoritly in India. Of the Sahitya Akademi, setup in 1954, Nehru was the first Chairman, but left all decisions to be taken by him, who was the Vice-Chairman. He also sought Radhakrishnan's opinion on matters of personnel in the government and administration.

Presiding over the sessions of the Rajya Sabha was the aspect of the Vice-Presidentship which had attracted Radhakrishnan the least. He look pride later in the fact that during his ten years as the chairman he had hardly missed the crucial period at the beginning of the day at any setting of the house. As the first chairman of the newly assembled Rajya Sabha, he took pains to build up conventions for its proper functioning. Representing as Vice-President of the Government of India, he attended all receptions at foreign embassies on national days and was present at official banquets hosted by the President or the Prime Minister. His translation of the *Upanishads*, with a long interpretative introduction and full notes was published in 1953. Two of his works, *Recovery of Faith* and *East and West* were published in 1955.

Towards the end of 1956 Radhakrishnan set off on a trip to the east which would have taken him to Indonesia, Japan and China; but he had to terminate it midway because of a sudden deterioration in the health of his wife. His wife passed away on 26 November 1956. In January 1955 Dr. Rajendra Prasad, on his own initiative, had written to the Prime Minister that, though his term as President had still two years to run, he would like to retire as he had completed five years in office. Towards the end of 1956, Azad spoke to Rajendra Prasad without Nehru's knowledge and asked him if he would agree to continue as President if requested. Rajendra Prasad replied that this was for Azad and other friends to decide, and Azad said he would speak to Nehru. On 23 March 1957 Nehru discussed with Rajendra Prasad for the first time the matter of the Presidentship. On 31 Mach 1957 at the meeting it was decided to request Radhakrishnan to continue as Vice-President for a second term. To Radhakrishnan this was a blow. He was tired of being minor royalty,with the added tedium of presiding over the Rajya Sabha, and was looking forward to winding up his career with five years as head of state. He replied to Nehru declining to serve as Vice-President. Pant called on Radhakrishnan to plead that he should continue in the national interest. Morarji Desai also requested Radhakrishnan to continue as Vice-President. Finally Radhakrishnan agreed to accept a second term.

The common setback in the choice of the President in 1957 drew Nehru and Radhakrishnan even closer together. The Prime Minister said he had never since 1947 been as depressed as he was now. Radhakrishnan regarded Nehru as the greatest single influence in the world for peace and all his own efforts were intended at a different level to support Nehru's policies. Internally too he was convinced that Nehru alone stood between the country and chaos. In May 1957, a week after Radhakrishnan's re-election as Vice-President, the Prime Minister suggested him to visit China. The visit to China itself Radhakrishnan could not have timed better. In his private talks with Mao, no immediate problems were raised; but there were some remarks of significance. Nehru also wanted him to visit the United States again and this he did in 1958. In Washington he met Eisenhower and Dulles. Radhakrishnan's main concern, in his talks with officials as well as in his public addresses, was to strengthen the prospects of peace by seeking understanding and drawing the attention of people in the United States to the better side of the Soviet Union.[7] In the summer of 1960, when Prasad went for two weeks on an official visit to the Soviet Union, the Prime Minister, citing the possible need for emergency measures in case of a general strike as the reason, had Radhakrishnan formally sworn in to discharge the duties of the President.

In 1962 Radhakrishnan was elected President by an overwhelming majority. He was the official Congress candidate. As President, he appeared almost too good to be true. Patrician and patriarchal, endowed with a noble face and trim figure, he dressed with dignity, carried himself with distinction, and performed the ceremonial duties of his office with the proper measure of gravitas. But he was always more than an ornamental figurehead.

An important figure in his own right, with a world-wide reputation as a philosophor, he was well-liked in all countries. Nehru approved of Radhakrishnan's forth rightness in public speech and, in private, sought his advice on matters important as well as minor. The British Academy, of which Radhakrishnan had been a Fellow since 1939, now elected him as Honorary Fellow, and the Government of India, on the request of the National Federation of Teachers, declared that his birthday, 5 September, would be celebrated every year as Teacher's

Day.

Radhakrishnan initiated the process of throwing open the gates of the President's palace in Delhi twice a week to whosoever might wish to present petitions or voice grievances, and these plaints were promptly passed on to the authorities concerned with a request for report on action taken. He continued his practice of travelling round the country and speaking on general issues. The close bonds between Radhakrishnan and Nehru also stretched to include Nehru's daughter. The press abroad took an interest in the possibility of building up the President as against the Prime Minister. Of even more importance to India were his visits to the United States and Britain. He spoke of the importance of non-alignment to the world and of India's commitment to democracy, freedom and the peaceful solution of international disputes.

The coverage of Radhakrishnan's speeches and broadcasts in the American press was not extensive mainly because hardly any of them were from a written text. *The New York Times*, while agreeing that he was emerging as a key personality on the Indian political scene, drew a sharper picture of confrontation with the Prime Minister and suggested that with Nehru's leadership of the Congress and government declining the centre of gravity has begun to shift to the President with his residual control in time of emergency over the military and the bureaucracy. With cataract developing on both eyes, his reading and writing were limited, and he spent more time than before, talking to visitors. On 23 May the home secretary called on the secretary to the President and told him that the Prime Minister was not well. On the morning of 27 May Indira Gandhi telephoned to Radhakrishnan to tell him that 'Father is not at all well'. Nehru had passed away at 1.50 p.m. After Nehru's death, Radakrishnan for the rest of his term was politically a lonely person. Then the election was held, Shastri was chosen leader, and Radhakrishnan accepted Nanda's resignation and administered to Shastri the oath of office as Prime Minister.

Radhakrishnan liked and respected Shastri, but obviously had little in common with him. Shastri was essentially a party organiser, diffident about succeeding Nehru, soon stricken by a heart attack and yet to carry all sections of his own party with him. Radhakrishnan's main effort at this time, was in the field of foreign policy. On 26 January 1965, fifteen years after the promulgation of the Constitution, Hindi became the official language of the union; and doubts arose as to whether the Shastri government would abide by Nehru's assurance that English would continue as an associate official language as long as the non-Hindi speaking people required it.

Radhakrishnan was not happy about the Tashkent declaration. Pakistan had not been obliged to settle the Kashmir problem by recognising the cease-fire line as an international boundary, and the line itself had not been improved by allotting to India the mountain passes which she had captured. Nor had Pakistan given binding assurances that she would not again send armed infiltrators into Kashmir. At 2.15 a.m. on 11 January 1966 Radhakrishnan was woken up to be told that Shastri had died at Tashkent of a massive heart attack about ten minutes before. There were four in the field—Nanda, Morarji Desai, Indira Gandhi and Yashwantrao Chavan. Indira Gandhi was Radhakrishnan's choice and he worked for her silently behind the scenes without compromising the dignity of his office. On 15 January eight chief ministers declared their support for Mrs Gandhi and, though the poll was to be four days later, the battle was as good as won.

Radhakrishnan's attitude to his new Prime Minister was affectionate, supportive—and non-serious. Having helped to secure Mrs Gandhi the office of Prime Minister, Radhakrishnan set out to train her to function adequately. From the start of her Prime Ministership foreign governments had looked to the President for counsel. The plain speaking on internal problems drew wide comment and some Congressmen complained to Mrs Gandhi about Radhakrishnan's criticisms. What they did not know was that he had shown her the text before recording and she had approved it. In the second half of 1966 Radhakrishnan was generally in a relaxed mood. He continued, though at an easier pace than before, his round of speaking engagements in various parts of the country and assisted in the preparation of a documentary film of his life. Though it was the last year of his term of office he gave no thought to what had already begun to interest some others—the possibility of his re-election.

On 4 December, while watching a private showing of a Telugu film, Radhakrishnan suddenly felt the fingers of his right hand go numb; and a litlle later he also had some difficulty with his speech. He had wanted to go on leave and request Zakir Husain to act as President but Indira Gandhi requested him not to precipitate matters. Although his recovery was rapid, he regarded this first sign of failing health as an indication that he should retire. The Congress Parliamentary Board met on 5April. Four members followed Mrs Gandhi and two went with Kamaraj and the final decision was left to be taken by the Prime Minister and the President of the party. Finally on 9 April, Radhakrishnan, after ringing Kamaraj to inform him that he had waited long enough, announced his decision not to allow his name to go forward and this came within minutes of the Chief Justice's consent to be a candidate, though the two decisions had nothing to do with each other. In his five years as the country's President, Radhakrishnan, without transgressing the letter or the spirit of the Constitution, set healthy precedents and built for the office a role in conforming national purpose and unity.[8]

In September 1973 Radhakrishnan slipped and broke his hip; and thereafter he was bedridden and began patently to break up. In the early hours of 17 April 1975, he drifted out of the harbour on a silent tide. The response of the common people was exemplified by the crowds that assembled at his death. They did not claim to comprehend his thought or even to understand his speeches and writings, which were all in English. But they knew that he had cared. So they came in their thousands and joined the well-to-do, the politicians and the diplomats in laying flowers on his body; and they then lined the route to the cremation.

REFERENCES

1. Gopal, S., *Radhakrishnan: A Biography*, pp. 13-53.
2. Radhakrishnan, S., *Eastern Religion and Western Thought*, p. 63.
3. Gopal, S., *op. cit.*, pp.76-83.
4. Radhakrishnan, S., *Religion and Society*, p. 87.
5. Gopal, S., *op. cit.*, pp. 94-136.
6. *Ibid.*, pp. 190-212.
7. *Ibid.*, pp. 238-292.
8. *Ibid.*, pp. 342-358.

2

ON EDUCATION

Radhakrishnan is one of the outstanding intellectuals of the twentieth century. Profound in his knowledge of philosophy and modern in his outlook, he interpreted the doctrines of Hindu religion in a manner easily understood by any educated man, in both the East and the West. He looked upon with an equal eye the achievements of scientists and the experience of mystics, saints and sages. He spoke and wrote in the English language. And the language was infinitely the richer for it. He was an educationist for the greater part of his life.

Radhakrishnan does not identify education with knowledge or regard it as a process of putting sight as it were into blind eyes but also maintains that we cannot be wise without some basis of knowledge. Education is a second birth to him. He said, "An initiation into the life of a spirit, a training of human souls in the pursuit of truth and the practice of virtue".[1] Education is a process of self-conquest. It will occur only if the individual himself makes steps to bring his inward nature to fulfilment. He conceives education to be liberating and life giving as it is meant to help a person overcome spiritual inertia and to promote sensitivity, which includes responsiveness to the problems and horrible plight of our fellowmen.[2] Education must prepare man to anticipate needs and meet new situations. It is universal and life-long. He said, "Education is a dynamic, life-long, pre-eminently self-propelled, emancipating and altruistic activity".[3] The educated man has an open mind, a broad outlook, is willing to reconsider issues and makes his own decisions.

Radhakrishnan endorses the Chinese adage that if you are planning for a hundred years, grow men as the quality of life depends on them. He thinks that education is necessary as long as any society is in need of progress or of social and economic reconstruction. It is meant to enable individuals to solve the problems of society. If a nation wants to avoid a parasitical existence, education is necessary in order to keep in the vanguard of development. It is necessary to provide the nation with leaders who are men of integrity.

The individual educational aims stress the needs and development of the individual while the social educational aims focus attention on the demands and necessities of society. Radhakrishnan considers the individual aims as important and they are like education for self-realisation, education for purpose, education for character formation, education for individuality and education of the whole man. The goal of education is self-knowledge. According to Radhakrishnan, in the absence of the inward restraint of conscience we are likely to become self-centred, irresponsible and abuse our freedom. He considers character formation to be an aim of importance which necessarily involves the practice of virtue. He said, "Compassion adds to the inner freedom of the individual and diminishes the load of psychological suffering and bondage weighing on man".[4] Education will be incomplete if it does not initiate the child to the supreme values of love, truth, goodness and beauty and fill him with a sense of purpose. He understands this purpose as the pursuit of truth and its application to improve human life.

Radhakrishnan advocates an all-round development of the individual. Education should not only train the intellect, promote technical skill but also develop a person's aesthetic abilities and especially moral and spiritual values. He observes that due to a lopsided emphasis on intellectual and material needs rare attention is paid to the refinement of the heart and discipline of the spirit. He opines that due importance must be given to the fruition of a person's uniqueness by detecting and developing his talents, observing and handling his limitations as well as by promoting the rights of the unfettered mind, which helps him to preserve his autonomy and prevents his complete socialisation. He thinks that development of the individual makes for his uniqueness and the unity of mankind.[5]

Man does not develop and function in a vacuum. He has the responsibility to make his contribution to the improvement of the social order. Individual freedom entails social responsibility. Education seeks to change the social order by promoting a healthy nationalism and the spirit of internationalism. Radhakrishnan thinks that education should work towards a citizenry that is enlightened, responsible and united. He also thinks that in order to work for national integration, diversity must be subordinated to unity, the basic truths of all religions, namely, the universality of the spirit, the inviolability of personality, the fact of fellowship, the duty of service and the power of sacrifice are to be practised. He opines that text-books should project a true image of the worthy elements of our culture, such as its rich spiritual content, its ability to renew itself and so on to rid patriotism of its half-truths and prejudices.

According to Radhakrishnan, "The two principle features of the modern world are that we are members of one another, and that there is no decree of God or man which compels us to be sick, hungry, poor and unemployed".[6] So certain problems in the world can be solved by a joint pooling of resources. He thinks that we should try to attain a unity of spirit before we can get together for political unity. The unity of spirit can be realised only through education. He said, "There is nothing national with regard to education. The different countries are provinces of a common republic of culture. Culture is international, science is cosmopolitan in its essence and reality".[7] He thinks that subjects like international relations, the study and appreciation of the achievements of the culture of different nations and an awareness of the work done by the UN and its agencies should be introduced as a part of every person's general education. He said, "All education is, on the one side a search for truth, on the other a pursuit of social betterment".[8] The aims of education are closely connected with the functions of educational institutions.

To Radhakrishnan, learning is a dynamic never-ending process which excites the individual's imagination, stimulates his reflective and critical faculties, enables him to anticipate needs and meet new situations. The function of the university is to blaze new paths and nourish new ideals. Independent thinking signifies relief from the burden of obsolete and inert ideas, from prejudices and mob passion fed to us by the media. He said, "The promotion of the freedom of thought is the ideal of the university. It has little to do with the protection of privilege or a call to conformity".[9] He regards the university as the custodian of culture and the critic of the social order. They should strive to be repositories of culture. According to Radhakrishnan, it is the university's function to keep the torch of culture ablaze although it can cause a conflagration or revolution. He thinks that if a culture is alive it will respond to challenges, be they physical, social or spiritual.

Radhakrishnan regards Indian culture as a palimpsest in which new characters do not entirely efface the old. He thinks that we have had a long tradition of austerity, renunciation, of education and service.

The university will have to hark back to the past, to discover and retain what is valuable in our heritage and shed what is ignoble in it. He thinks that the university in its function of reshaping society has to adopt the via media of constructive conservatism which brings a blend between traditional values and modern knowledge. He agrees with the view that the university has the task of training students for leadership both for public life and for the various professions. The university must discriminate between wise and dangerous leadership. He thinks that the performance of future leaders is bound to be coloured by the behaviour of their mentors at the university.

The university has to work for the propagation of peace. According to Radhakrishnan, the university can do this by trying to overcome racial pride, religious intolerance and the lust for power. He regards teaching and research as complementary pursuits. He thinks that research is needed for the modernisation of our agriculture, industry, for the maintenance of public health and also for the conservation of what is best in our culture. He appreciates the utility value of research in the applied fields. He said, "The university members should manifest understanding, sympathy and strive to promote justice, equality and fraternity and in dealing with problems the university man should be unattached without being unconcerned, unambitious without being indolent, warm-hearted without being sentimental".[10]

Radhakrishnan is against the university adopting an ivory-tower approach but considers that it should be a service centre which strives by hard work and sacrifice to eliminate inequality. He maintains that education must have a vocational bias at the secondary and university level. Vocational education is necessary for both the individual and society as it needs scientists, technologists to contribute to the fund of knowledge, to eradicate poverty and to make economic progress. In his works, he refers to professional education rather than vocational or technical education. To him, professional education entails not only the acquisition of knowledge and technical skills but also a sense of social responsibility and respect for moral values. He thinks that vocational preparation should commence as soon as the child shows a craving or aptitude for it. He is aware that the area of vocational education is bristling with problems. His advice to the educated unemployed is that they should be prepared to take up any job and do it well. He considers it the school's business to dispel wrong ideas and attitudes towards superior and inferior education and to instil the idea of the dignity and relative value of all work. He concedes that specialisation is necessary in our age of rapid expansion of knowledge. He opines that the university has the stupendous task of moulding the character of the young, of preparing them both for the life and livelihood.[11]

Radhakrishnan believes that lack of self-control results in a deterioration of standards of learning and scholarship, in self-centredness and lack of compassion. The student's task of study and reflection demands intellectual sincerity, dedication, hard work and sacrifice. The entire educational enterprise revolves round the students, who are both the builders and the material of the new structure. He said, "Truth or repose, it has been said, you may take which you please, you never can have both".[12] He advocates that students should fight social evils, injustice and protest against religious fanaticism. The student must also render service. He said, "Though students should engage in protest and action in the social field and take a proper interest in elections and good government it does not mean that they have to engage in party politics, in immature political activity when they ought to be preparing themselves for life's struggles".[13]

Student misbehaviour springs from several sources. It is due to a person's self-centredness, malice and idleness or is the outcome of surplus energy or because of a lack of opportunity, poor living conditions and financial worries. A fall in academic standards, lack of student motivation, tensions generated by examinations and lack of support from parents in matters of student misbehaviour are also reasons that Radhakrishnan gives for student indiscipline. It may be due to loss of integrity and moral purpose, authoritarian methods of imposing discipline, poor teaching methods, lack of personal relationship between the teachers and the taught. He thinks that sometimes bright students get restless and consequently unruly because several of their classmates are not able to cope with the studies.

The teacher is the cornerstone of the arch of education. Success of the educational process depends considerably on the teacher, for it is the teacher who has to implement aims, and to build the character of the students. Radhakrishnan says that at bottom, the quality of a university is always in direct proportion to the quality of its teachers. A good teacher is one who knows his subject, is enthusiastic about it and one who never ceases to learn. He said, "A good teacher has a sense of commitment to his work, derives satisfaction from it and is not prompted to do things for fame or power. Above all, he is a man who loves his students".[14] The good teacher is one who is objective, just, humble and is open to correction. He is aware that in real life, teachers are not paragons of virtue or models of intellectual efficiency, so he cautions that students should imitate only the blameless acts of their mentors.

The teacher's main function is to transmit the intellectual and ethical heritage to the young which presupposes that he has knowledge of both facts and values and is aware of the assets and limitations of our culture and tradition. He will try to remove the leaden weights of pride and prejudice, passion and desire which are likely to cloud a student's vision. Radhakrishnan is adamant that the teacher should get students to think for themselves by placing before them the best of what has been thought and said and then leaving them free to decide for themselves, by discouraging hero worship wherein the educator is blindly obeyed, by promoting alertness of mind and moral restraint so that the person judges for himself and acts on his own convictions. So he would prefer the use of tutorials and seminars, which offer scope for intellectual midwifery although he maintains that teaching should be adopted to suit the psychological needs and interests of the learner. The quest for new knowledge is a vital function of the university and therefore of the teacher.[15]

Radhakrishnan is totally opposed to the prevailing spoon-feeding techniques of teaching and methods. The data fed to the students is often stale and stereotyped and tends to devitalise teaching and to kill interest. He is aware that since industry offer better salary than teaching, the university does not attract the best people. He maintains that the factors responsible for the denigration of the teacher must be removed. P. Altbach said, "Some teacher politicians and administrators with little or no interest in academic matters secure lucrative positions for themselves whilst those devoted to scholarship go unnoticed and unrewarded".[16]

Radhakrishnan suggests that selection of staff for universities should be on the basis of academic distinction, teaching ability, leadership in student activities. He thinks that promotions of staff should not be on the basis of mere seniority but on an evaluation of the individual's achievement. As regards retirement he thinks that whilst the usual retirement age is sixty, teachers should be allowed to continue even till sixty-five so long as their intellectual capacity is unimpaired. Teachers working conditions have to be improved by providing them with a good library, equipment, a book grant, smaller classes and better salaries so that they will be able to devote themselves to university work. He thinks that the state should not be niggardly in providing finance to the university as it is an asset to the country.[17]

Radhakrishnan acknowledges the role that the environment, especially the media, has in educating the child. He thinks in the past political and religious authorities used education to propagate their ideologies and the same could be done more efficiently today through the media. We can expand our knowledge through the media. He regards films as the most popular of all the media. He opines that film-makers have the responsibility not just to entertain the people but to raise cultural standards, to promote thought on noble ideals, to stir the depths of our being, and discipline our nature. Films can be an effective force in bringing about national integration, in breaking down barriers of caste and age-old prejudices. He holds that some films have led to an increase in the rate of crime, they are likely to cloud our judgement as the data projected on the screen appeals to the emotions rather than to reason.

Science aims at the pursuit of truth, which is no different from the philosophical ideal of the vision of reality. Hence the scientific approach is moral since the scientist carries on his investigations in an attitude of freedom from prejudice and hospitality to new ideas. Radhakrishnan said, "Not only does science provide man with a knowledge of his natural and social environment but the scientific method is valuable in any investigation as the student learns to distinguish knowledge from opinion, to weigh evidence, to state and examine an opponent's view objectively".[18] Again, he said, "Science frees us from the tyranny of words by taking us to the things itself and is likely to make us precise in our use of language".[19] It has enabled mankind to battle with ignorance, with disease, with poverty. It provides us with the tools of civilisation but not with guidance for their use. All sciences give us knowledge not judgement, power not vision, strength not sanction. He observes that a scientific study of social phenomena may lead one to uphold a determinist view of history which looks upon social growth as obedience to some laws. He focuses attention on the dangers of a curriculum which attaches undue importance to scientific and technical studies to the exclusion of other vital interests.

The study of humanities is necessary because man does not know how to use the knowledge and resources at his command. Radhakrishnan opines that philosophy, religion and literature, which embody the wisdom of the ages are necessary because they interpret the higher laws of the universe and are more likely to bring us wisdom. It is the university's job to produce not only trained scientists and experts but also compassionate men. Philosophy gives man a frame of reference which provides direction and meaning to life. It enables man to liberate himself from attachment to material goods, etc. For Radhakrishnan, philosophy is not just an esoteric study nor is it the mere possession of a technique but it is an activity of examining life by doubting and thinking courageously.

The bond between philosophy and literature is that both of them keep up the mind's cherished gift of dream and imagination. Radhakrishnan felt that the literary artist should adopt a via media between realism which mirrors life and romanticism which describes utopias. He said, "The writer should aim not just at stability but should produce a ferment since true literature has always spearheaded change and contributed to cultural progress".[20] Literature can provide hope to a sick generation because it arouses compassion in man. It is instrumental in combating ignorance, prejudice and psychological stress. He thinks that literature can help establish the world community based on the brotherhood of the spirit. Great literature is universal in its appeal and endures forever. He believed that literature is the result of a writer's intense experience or his travail of the spirit and the paradox is that whilst the literary genius resembles all, no one resembles him. It can flourish only in freedom.

Radhakrishnan contends that the content of education would be woefully inadequate if it did not include the arts. He opines that art is required to develop the creative imagination and give people vision. Art appeals not just to the senses or the mind, but to the spirit. Its language is universal and it is valued for all time. To him, art not only creates an atmosphere of beauty but it also enhances our ability to enjoy beauty. He tells us that though the artist speaks of different moods of laughter, pity, anger, love, they are all variations of a common theme, *karuna*, compassion, love with suffering. Art is not different from worship or from religion for it occurs only when heaven touches earth. All great art is an overflow of contemplation, chastity, emotional intensity and heightened vision.

Radhakrishnan's contention is that in imparting education, one must not lose sight of the unity of knowledge. The basis for the unity of knowledge consists in the fact that all fields of knowledge are concerned with truth and beauty, are based on faith and aim at dispelling ignorance, prejudice and unfounded belief. He thinks that all subjects require to be harnessed to the science of the spirit. He said, "Science and the humanities converge into a single whole, each portraying a facet with a colour of its own, yet each reflecting something of the rest".[21] He thinks that wisdom is more easily gained through the study of literature, philosophy and religion.

Radhakrishnan attaches considerable importance to the personal contact between the teacher and the student. He views the ideal teacher as a person who inspires the student by his character, by devotion to his work. He regards religion as an essential means to the fulfilment of man as a spiritual being and so considers the communication of religion as a definite task of all educational institutions. He explains that though we do not favour dogmatic or sectarian religion, to be secular is not to be religiously illiterate. He thinks that religion should be accorded great value in the educational process because Indian tradition has always felt the need to explore man's inner life, to ponder on some imponderables such as beauty and mystery of the universe. He is dissatisfied with the prevailing method of teaching religion. He holds that on no account should religious instruction engage in competitive indoctrination. All schools must teach the universal truths of all religions.[22]

Radhakrishnan suggests that an environment of religious vitality may be fostered by making morning meditation an integral part of college life. He advocates the reading of books on the lives of great men, be they thinkers, artists, saints or social reformers. A reverent study of the essentials of all religions would also be satisfying. He insists on the study of classics. A study of the classics is likely to widen a person's perspective on life, to cast out narrow and sectarian interests and unite man in the realisation of their humanity. He acknowledges that the idea of 'Education through the Study of Great Books' is not new. He agrees that since society is or tends to be acquisitive and mechanistic, man has to preserve his essential spiritual nature through meditation and the study of the classics.

The current spiritual impoverishment is due to man's lack of self-control, the spread of scientific positivism, and the ineffectiveness of religion. Radhakrishnan said, "Mechanisation and speed have led to dehumanisation and together with the passivity induced by the media have made man no better than performing animals".[23] He thinks that the teaching fraternity must accept responsibility for the intellectual inadequacy and spiritual illiteracy of those whom we produce, for their acquiescence in social injustices and for their failure to fight social evils. He said, "It is for the university to make the soul . . . to provide an outlook on life that is reverent to the eternal values and responsive to temporal events".[24] To him, the chief defects of our educational system are: (1) an unholy reverence for authority with the consequent surrender of our critical faculties, (2) a loss of quality due to the phenomenal expansion in higher education, (3) alienation of degree holders from the vast majority who are underprivileged, and (4) utility-oriented education with loss of its spiritual dimension and stress on specialisation which, though needed, is not without its dangers.

Educational opportunities should be given to all, particularly those who hail from a poor social background. Higher education gives a new view of life and a new set of values. The devaluation of education has led to student unrest. Indian higher education has resulted in a dual culture. Suri said, "Democratic pressure for higher education has produced an undemocratic situation in which mass education has lagged behind."[25] Radhakrishnan opines that education is the right of every individual and it is not a privilege of the nobility, gentry or professional classes. So no one should be denied education on grounds of caprice, prejudice, favouritism nor should anyone be discriminated against on grounds of religion, community or language. He clarifies that in a democracy educational opportunity for citizens does not mean identical opportunities, for individuals differ in gifts and interests.

Radhakrishnan is aware that the portals of the university are closed to a great number who are economically backward. He suggests that there should be a generous system of scholarships to remove economic barriers to enable any child to climb to the limit of his capacity. He is aginst unrestricted expansion at the university level as it leads to a steep fall in standards of education. He believes in an aristocracy of direction and forthrightly proclaims that exceptional ability is socially so valuable that it may be given exceptional opportunity. He is opposed to unlimited expansion in the institutions of higher education because he thinks that bigness is almost necessarily fatal to greatness. He opines that only one-third of the seats should be allotted to the backward communities for a period of ten years and the remaining should be given to all on the basis of an open competition. He suggests that students who seek admission in college should be mature enough to use the opportunities given to them. He suggests that in the case of students who attend evening classes the duration of such courses should be extended so that there is no fall in standards. He opines that every person should receive education to suit his talents and interests.[26]

Radhakrishnan thinks that a purposive attempt must be made simultaneously to provide people with an ethical and cultural education. He appreciates Gandhi's basic education programme. He thinks that an educational system must be responsive to human needs and values and must not become fixed or conventional. He also thinks that rural clinics, rural library service, agricultural extension work and cooperative banking could help to improve the quality of life in the village and could become part of the secondary school training programme. He opines that it is a mistaken idea to regard practical work as inferior. He thinks that information about the work done by agricultural colleges should be disseminated to the farmers.

Radhakrishnan thinks that the approach to linguistic differences should not be doctrinaire but pragmatic. Though a common language would be useful, it is not possible to adopt a single language for the whole country due to the different nature of our people. He has not given criteria for one language as the medium of instruction because he thinks that in view of our rich variety. This is not possible. He agrees that English satisfies the criteria and on account of its comprehensiveness and international status it is necessary that university students should be proficient in it. He proposes the three language formula which recognises the claims and limitations of the local, national and international language. He thinks that general education should be in the vernacular for it incarnates the genius of the people.

REFERENCES

1. Radhakrishnan, S., *The Report of the University Education Commission*, Vol. I, p. 17.
2. Radhakrishnan, S., *Faith Renewed*, p. 24.
3. Radhakrishnan, S., *Education, Politics and War*, p. 106.
4. Radhakrishnan, S., *Speeches and Writings*, p. 180.
5. Rodrigues, C., *The Social and Political Thought of Dr. S. Radhakrishnan*. pp. 122-123.
6. Radhakrishnan, S., *True Knowledge*, p. 74.
7. Radhakrishnan, S., *Education, Politics and War*, p. 67.
8. Radhakrishnan, S., *True Knowledge*, p. 63.
9. Radhakrishnan, S., *Freedom and Culture*, p. 4.
10 Radhakrishnan, S., *Occasional Speeches and Writings*, p. 160
11. Rodrigues, C., *op. cit.*, pp. 128-130
12. Radhakrishnan, S., *Freedom and Culture*, p. 34.
13. *Ibid.*, p. 127
14. Radhakrishnan, S., *True Knowledge*, p. 34.
15. Rodrigues, C., *op. cit.*, pp. 133-134.

16. Altbach. P., *The Academic Profession*, p. 13.
17. Rodrigues. C., *op. cit.*, p 135.
18. Radhakrishnan. S., *Freedom and Culture*, p. 24.
19. Radhakrishnan. S., *True Knowledge*, p. 53.
20. *Ibid.*, p. 47.
21. Radhakrishnan. S., *Speeches and Writings*, p. 120.
22. Rodrigues. C., *op. cit.*, pp. 142-143
23. Radhakrishnan. S., *Occasional Speeches and Writings*, p. 205
24. Radhakrishnan. S., *Education, Politics and War*, p. 175.
25. Suri. S., *Education or Catastrophe*, p. 100.
26. Rodrigues. C., *op cit.*, pp. 147-149.

3

ON RELIGION AND PHILOSOPHY

At times Radhakrishnan has been described as nothing more than 'a liaison officer' in philosophy between the East and the West. He has also been characterised as a historian of philosophy and not a philosopher himself. Rightly understood, the above partial characterisation of Radhakrishnan need not necessarily be construed as negative or pejorative. One could be a first-rate philosopher without ceasing to be a historian of philosopher. Secondly, one could be both an interpreter and a philosopher at the same time. He adores some deity or other, his *guru* and the tradition to which he belongs. Interestingly enough, swearing by the name of *guru* he criticises him, goes beyond him, and at times even demolishes him. He has philosophised in the grand Indian tradition, criticising his teachers, following them interrogatively and reconstructing them creatively.[1]

Radhakrishnan rightly claims and emphasises the originality of his interpretation based on what he calls his own spiritual experience. He said, "Although I admire the great masters of thought, ancient and modern, Eastern and Western, I cannot say that I am a follower of any, accepting his teaching in its entirety. I do not suggest that I refused to learn from others or that I was not influenced by them. While I was greatly stimulated by the minds of all those whom I have studied, my thought does not comply with any fixed traditional pattern. For my thinking had another source and proceeded from my own experience, which is not quite the same as what is acquired by mere study and reading. It is born of spiritual experience rather than deduced from logically ascertained premises. Philosophy is produced more by our encounter with reality than by the historical study of such encounters".[2]

Influenced by two different traditions of religion and philosophy, Indian-Hindu and Western-Christian, Radhakrishnan felt deeply stirred within. He is concerned with Indian thought as something which is alive. His interpretation of Indian culture in general and its philosophy in particular is not mechanical but a creative transformation of the same. He distances himself from the false one which telescopes the present into the past, the present historian's thinking into the past thought. He pleads for 'intellectual unselfishness or humility' on the part of the historian of philosophy.

Accused of abstract metaphysical and nebulous idealism in our modern age which is so marked by violence, poverty and ruthless suppression of human rights, Radhakrishnan actually uses his own interests and *jijnasa* to lend meaning to his understanding of the history of Indian philosophy, or to be more accurate, that of Indian culture itself. What disturbs him most is the confusion of thought and the resulting scepticism of millions of men. He said, "My one supreme interest has been to try to restore a sense of spiritual values to the millions of religiously displaced persons, who have been struggling to find precarious refuges in emergency camps of Art and Science, of Fascism and Nazism, of Humanism and Communism".[3] To him, art, science and the different forms of totalitarianism are all emergency camps for refugees.

Radhakrishnan was deeply influenced by Tagore, Gandhi and Sri Aurobindo. In his *Religion of the Spirit* one hears the distinct echoes of Tagore's *The Religion of Man*, Gandhi's Hindu *Dharma*, and Sri Aurobindo's The religion of Humanity. He is opposed to the purely philosophical or intellectual ideal of humanism. This word has been used by so many thinkers and in so many different senses that unless it is sufficiently clarified one's more commitment to it does not mean much. He is not in favour of the mere social, i.e. secular form, of humanism. He believes that the social form of humanism rests on a deeper spiritual truth. The form of humanism which is a mere reaction against fascism and communism is false and therefore rejected by him. He defends the true form of humanism in which human individuality and dignity are quite consistent with social unity and harmony. Individuals shed their egoism, transcend their narrowness and find their larger self in the society.[4]

Radhakrishnan's 'religion of the spirit' is not opposed to scientific temper. Rather, it is integral to it. He is opposed to credal religion. His concept of the religion of the spirit, special significance is attached to the freedom of the spirit. 'Spirit' is always 'spirit of' something or of some being. Both thing and being have their body, gross or subtle. In a way, spirit is the freedom of the body. One must draw a distinction between two expressions, 'freedom of body' and 'freedom from body'. He highlights the former, which recognises body as the locus of freedom. This is his way of dispelling the widespread misconception that spirituality means negation of materialism. He not only affirms materialism, but he also asserts the positive character and relevance of Marxism in the present day context.

Radhakrishnan draws an important line of distinction between the Religion of Authority and the Religion of the Spirit. The Religion of Authority is basically institutional, must have its unquestionable scripture, spiritual head, and some prescribed rites and rituals. He reiterates the Indian view of the Religion of the Spirit. One must try to realise the significance of his concern for the universality of the true religion. The Religion of the Spirit is not to be taken as a religion among religions. In a sense, it is really unique. First, because it is not revealed. Secondly, because it is not committed to a particular scripture and guided by an unquestionable spiritual head. Thirdly, because it does not reject non-religious forms of knowledge and values, like scientific temper and technological efficacy. Fourthly, because he defends this religion against the criticism of other worldliness. It is life-affirming, world-affirming, and concerned with human misery, war, peace and politics, and yet it symbolises the human aspiration for the transcendent, for the perfection yet to be achieved, for the progress yet to be made.[5]

Radhakrishnan's idea of religion is not even remotely inconsistent with the science. Explaining the point, he draws our attention to the fact that the true religious man, like the scientist, is expected to show a critical questioning spirit. He must not accept anything merely on the basis of authority. This enables him to rise above the narrow confines of his class-interest, national chauvinism and religious egoism. True religion is all-inclusive.

For Radhakrishnan, religion is the supreme achievement of man's profound experience. It is the deepest kind of life reflecting the different phases, complex and conflicting, of human living and there is no future for man apart from the religious dimension. He said, "The history of religion is the record of the conflicts of contradictory systems, each of them claiming dogmatic finality and absolute truth, a claim made apparently absurd by the plurality of claimants".[6] Again, he said, "While the economic and political forces are bringing people close together, religions are doing their utmost to maintain the inner barriers that divide and antagonise peoples. . . . Religion engenders a great love for a great hate".[7]

Radhakrishnan calls himself an idealist. He explains what he means by this in *An Idealist View of Life*, which has been described as his mature and most significant work. An idealist view, says Radhakrishnan, finds that the universe has meaning, has value. Ideal values are the dynamic forces, the driving power of the universe. He said, "The idealist tradition both in the East and the West has asserted the supremacy of spirit in man".[8] His own idealist position is a creative restatement of the basic categories of *Advaita Vedanta*. He consistently interprets Hinduism, other religions and the nature of religion itself from the standpoint of *Advaita*. *Advaita*, often referred to by the generic term *Vedanta*, represents the essence of Hinduism. He said, "the germinal conceptions of Hinduism are contained in the *Vedanta* standard . . . The *Vedanta* is not a religion, but religion itself in its most universal and deepest significance".[9]

Radhakrishnan shares Vivekananda's belief in the immutable essence of religion, the basic oneness of existence and the essential unity of all religions. He maintains in his philosophical writings that he seeks above all to convey his insight into the meaning and purpose of life in order to provide a coherent and consistent interpretation of the world and to promote the religion of the spirit. As far as the meaning and purpose of life is concerned, he conceives of it as the gradual revelation of the divine or the eternal in man. Man's inner self is akin to the supreme; it mirrors the divine. In the depth of man's spiritual experience, the barriers between the self and ultimate reality fall away and the isomorphism of God's spirit and man's spirit is revealed.

For Radhakrishnan, spiritual life may be regarded as the completion or fulfilment of human life, and the ultimate goal of the cosmic process may be seen as the establishment of a spiritual kingdom of free spirits. The implication of this spiritual view of the universe is that it is impossible for the world to be regarded as illusory in any way, since it is the manifestation of God or the Divine Spirit, and hence real rather than illusory. But, as Radhakrishnan is at pains to point out, its reality is dependent rather than absolute; it is not ultimately real, which is precisely what the doctrine of *maya* seeks to convey. The world depends on the immanent activity of God, without which it would cease to be. It is a particular manifestation of divine, creative activity, but is mutability and eventual dissolution does not affect the absolute reality of God in any way. That is, the world may be dependent on God, but God is not dependent on the world.[10]

Radhakrishnan acknowledges that each religion takes its own path to the realisation of the goal of union with the divine, but insists that they are at one in their essence and in what is eternal in them. To him, religion is one in essence. Knowledge of the primordial form of religion is the result of an immediate, intuitive apprehension of the nature of ultimate reality, which in turn is the result of *jnana*, gnosis, or integral insight. It is a state of ecstasy; it is what is meant by saying that one is with God, and is an experience common to all religions. Hence, the importance of learning about the basic principles of all the great religions of the world.

The main aim of religion, according to Radhakrishnan, is to deliver man from meaninglessness and to give him eternal status. The dream of all the great religions of the world is to divinise the life of man. This is the *moksha* of the Hindus, the *nirvana* of the Buddhists, the kingdom of heaven of the Christians. He favours mono-religion, or the one, in the sense of a primordial, transcendental essence of religion, yet not to the exclusion of polyreligion, or the many historical forms of religion. Different religions are different paths to the realisation of the same goal of union with the divine, but they are all in essence one. In his view, the Hindu faith is not to be equated with dogmatism; its distinctive characteristic is inconsistence on the inward life of the spirit, for in man's inner-self, at the centre of his being, is that which is akin to the divine and the essence of reality, which is precisely what the *Upanisadic* aphorism *tat tvām asi* affirms.

Radhakrishnan considers religion to be the lifeblood of civilisation. To him, the decline of religion can be attributed to some internal and external factors. He is not in favour of preserving the exclusive character of each religion so that all souls are not driven to one spiritual enclosure. He said, "If we believe in blood, race and soil, our world will be filled with Belsems and Buchenwalds—If we believe in universal spiritual values, peace and understanding will grow".[11] Poor religious leadership and indifference to the problems and woes of mankind are the other factors for the decline of religion. He said, "On the supreme issues of peace, war, religions have been hesitant and complacent, if not militant and reactionary".[12] Creed, code and cult are the essential elements of every religion. It is only when they are abused that we have a religion that is ethically repugnant, content with metaphysical subtleties, academic abstractions, dogmatic conformity, ceremonial piety and group loyalties.

The external factors that have led to the eclipse of religion are developments in science, philosophy and the general temper of the age. Radhakrishnan is aware that science has helped man to gain increasing control over nature. Men worship at the laboratory rather than at the altar. But he does not regard science as a panacea for man's problems. He said, "Even with reference to physical nature, scientific knowledge does not give us inner truth. The measurable aspects are not the only ones".[13] So he said, "The positivist approach liberates us from religious obscurantism, it should not become a scientific obscurantism which distorts science itself by imposing on it wrong ideas of exactitude and verification".[14] He agrees with Tennant that both science and religion need faith, as proof is not possible in every case. The achievements of science bear witness to the spirit in man and science, properly understood, is spiritual in temper and leadings. He said, "Religion should not end in wars and inquisitions nor science in Hiroshimas and Nagasakis".[15]

Radhakrishnan takes pains to indicate that reason is not wholly devoid of faith and that the illumination of the mind and purification of the heart cannot be separated in the spiritual experience. He admits that religious faith reveals an aspect of human nature that is deeper than the intellect, so while philosophy is the love of wisdom, religion is the wisdom of love. The decline and ferment in religion are also due partly to the spirit of the age. He agrees with Santayana that scepticism which is said to be the chastity of the intellect, riddles the faith of yesterday and prepares us for the faith of tomorrow.[16]

For Radhakrishnan, the atheist is one who denies an idea of God but not God himself and neither agnosticism not atheism signify irreligious behaviour and outlook. He said, "Many atheists who say they do not believe in God act as if they did and there are many religious people who say they believe in God and act as if they did not. So militant atheism is an answer to dishonest religion".[17]

Humanism as a religion is deficient because it overlooks the immortal longings, the intimations of sanctity, the hunger and thirst for holiness, the readiness to suffer persecution and martyrdom. Radhakrishnan warns that a self-sufficient humanism can lead to an acquiescence in the merely practicable but material prosperity, and social service cannot make for happiness unless the latter is done in a self-sacrificing spirit. To him, communism may be regarded as a heresy in Christianity which protests against Christian or orthodoxy but which upholds Christian truth and principles.

According to Radhakrishnan, true religion is the religion of the spirit. It is a quest for self-realisation, an inner personal experience, an individual relation with the Divine. It is not worship but a way of becoming, of liberation. He upholds the value of asceticism which stands for renunciation of worldly goods, the control of one's desires but it should not lead to social quietism or else the ascetics are comparable to cut flowers in metal vases, beautiful to behold but which soon fade for lack of nourishment from the soul. So he advocates that a life of contemplation and withdrawal must be accompanied by an identification with the current of life, a participation in creative advance wherein mankind is lifted to a higher level.

To Radhakrishnan, religion is not just an intellectual conviction, nor is it merely an ecstatic feeling or social service. It embraces the whole of man's being. He said, "Religion as the experience of Reality is a movement of the whole self to the daily challenge of actual human relations, not belief in a set of propositions".[18] Religion is not an opiate for it is not a way out of life but a way into life. It is not an a academic discipline but a mystery to be lived. He condemns mere externalism and does not insist on obedience to laws and ordinances. He thinks that a distinction must also be made between eternal truths and accidental accretions. He is opposed to proselytism because the kernel of truth of every religion is universal and changeless.

True religion is universal and not parochial. According to Radhakrishnan, true religion is characterised by a reconciling spirit in that it is compatible not only with the spirit of science and the ethics of humanism but also with the universality of the ultimate truths proclaimed by various faiths. He thinks that a regimented mind is ill-suited for spiritual purposes. Spiritual religion or Religion of the Spirit signifies an atmosphere of freedom, growth of the divine in man which is visible in the love and service of man. He holds that the practice of the presence of God is the highest religion. He regards religion as more of a transforming experience than a notion of God. He defines religion both with and without God. He denounced dogmatic creeds and infallible beliefs yet he acknowledges that beliefs are the codified expressions of experience. He maintains that to sever a man from his religious ethos is like trying to separate gold from the rock in which it is embedded. He thinks that to love one's neighbour is not to compel him to share our opinions but to renounce one's own standards and see with the other man's eyes, feel with his heart and understand with his mind.[19]

Radhakrishnan is fully justified in decrying forced conversions, which certainly infringe on another person's liberty, yet there is no reason why a person who does not find his faith to be authentic enough should not be at liberty to renounce his faith if he chooses to do so. He stresses the need of bringing about a harmony of religions without destroying their identity and, at the same time, he does not rule out an assimilation of faiths. His Spiritual Religion has much in common with Neo-Hinduism. The influence of Hinduism on his concept of Spiritual Religion is visible in his stress on contemplation, tolerance, the basic quality of all religions and on religion being more a way of life than a form of thought. His idea of true religion reveals his understanding and appreciation of other faiths, especially Christianity. He has been very much influenced by Christianity in rejecting quietism for he constantly reiterates that the mystical basis of Hinduism is to be vitally linked with active involvement in the world's problems. He is aware that some have become disillusioned with religion because of its chaotic state.

Religion is indispensable to man as it satisfies man's basic need of worship, of his compelling and perennial need to encounter and come to terms with the unseen. Radhakrishnan believes that the need for faith is natural and inescapable. He said, "The age of faith is always with us, only the object of our faith changes".[20] Religion is of immeasurable value to the individual as it serves as a bridle to control man's nature. Religion awakens man to his spiritual penury and pride and calls for an attitude of humility. He is aware that a number of customs, institutions associated with Hindu *dharma* like *sati*, animal sacrifice, female infanticide, the *devadasi* system and untouchability are oppressive and should be abolished. He stresses that in serving suffering humanity we must not forget our spiritual moorings or the source from which altruism is derived. It binds men in a fellowship by giving them a spiritual outlook and in the past it has proved to be a great cohesive force in society. He said, "Any serious pursuit of ideas, any search after conviction, any adventure after virtue, arises from resources whose name is religion".[21] So religion is the main spring of both the individual and social life and is not doomed to die. All religions should be viewed with serenity and sympathy.

The universal religion that Radhakrishnan advocates is not syncretist in nature but seeks to preserve the identity and uniqueness of all religions. So no single religion by itself can be the basis for the spiritual unity of mankind but the goal should be to work for the Fellowship of Faiths, which he thinks is possible because religions today are less intransigent than before. Radhakrishnan is not in favour of a fusion of faiths into a synthetic creed for the religions of the world. He thinks that to stress religious diversity at the cost and neglect of spiritual unity would be philosophically unjustifiable, morally indefensible and socially dangerous. He speaks not only of a unity in diversity but also of a diversity that unites. He said, "The dream of a world society with a universal religion of which the historical faiths are but branches".[22]

Radhakrishnan thinks that in today's destructive world, religion is man's hope for survival and an instrument for peace. Hence religious harmony can pave the way for social harmony, and the direction for it lies in highlighting the common elements of all religions and working for a fellowship of faiths, in adopting an attitude of tolerance, in promoting an interest and understanding of comparative religions and in the influence wielded on humanity by religious leaders. The common elements which he thinks can make men more conscious of the transcendent unity underlying the empirical diversity of religions are: (a) all religions testify to the divine possibilities inherent in man; (b) to realise them we have to wrestle with the forces of waywardness within us; (c) God does not withhold his truth, His love and His grace from anyone; (d) religious experience is universal; (e) all religions uphold virtuous conduct; and (f) all of them stress the importance and significance of prayer wherein mankind seeks God and which is also proof of the universal revelation of God.[23]

Radhakrishnan advocates tolerance as a necessary ingredient for a fellowship of faiths. He thinks that in this respect India has a lot to teach the world for she has had a long history and tradition of tolerance. Tolerance is the homage which the finite mind pays to the inexhaustibility of the Infinite. He said, "Tolerance is not to be equat with pity, with condescension, not the abandonment and indiffere to truth. But it is co-existence which is to be manifested in love w culminates in brotherhood, and appreciation of other faiths".[24] Tho he is tolerant, he is intolerant of all creeds though equality of religio tolerance and mystical experience are indirectly the dogmas of his religion.

Secularism does not mean the denial and rejection of the Supreme. Radhakrishnan said, "It involves a recognition of spiritual realities not by abstention from the world, but by bringing to its life, its business and its pleasure, the controlling power of spiritual faith".[25] It does not mean the worship of a crass materialism. It signifies that the society and the state promote and encourage the coexistence, cooperation and mutual respect for religions. He has not discussed the problems of secularism, the difficulty of implementing the principle of state-religion separation, the presence of religious tensions and traces of religious fanaticism. These problems are largely due to the fact that no religion is without bigots and Indian religions are no exception.

Comparative religion throws light on the growth of religious consciousness and helps to break down the barriers of exclusivism which results in hostility and brings about tolerance which does not smack of a conscious superiority, condescending charity and patronising pity. Radhakrishnan thinks that Eastern religions are superior to the Western ones in being non-dogmatic and spiritually well-mannered for they do not condemn the good simply because it is not the best. They lay more emphasis on contemplation, on the development of the inner life and spiritual culture than on scholastic learning. Western religions have emphasised theological dogmatism, and looked with disdain on other faiths because of their exclusiveness. He contends that both types of religion are needed. They complement each other for religion is not only a life transcending ideal but also a life transforming faith. He contends that Christianity has wrestled with many social wrongs and has been responsible for the abolition of slavery but, by and large, Christians have closed their eyes to their own defects.

Radhakrishnan has always been referred to as a philosopher. He exemplifies the original meaning of philosophy, which in Greece meant 'love of wisdom'. A lover of wisdom, yes. By his elegantly simple style, he made his readers lovers of wisdom too. He never shed his *pundit's* touch in his dress, or even in the delivery of his speeches. There were no dramatic silences, whispers, sudden flights of fancy. Whether on stage or at his writing desk, his language flowed with an unhurried pace. It never ascended to the feverish pitch of a visionary prophet, nor descended to the style of a street-corner preacher. He spoke and wrote as he was: a man of erudition and common-sense; a person who could think and analyse and come down to the intellectual level of his listener-reader only to raise him to his own higher level; an ideal teacher; a man of gentle humour and unadvertised compassion.

Self- criticism had a vital role in Radhakrishnan's philosophy since he believed in a conscious effort to reach perfection, to achieve the spiritual way of life. His own life as a successful academic, able administrator, a dependable interpreter and a logically organised philosopher, is eloquent proof of his philosophy of life. This too he stated in his autobiographical fragment, emphasising the need for spiritual literacy if mankind wished to progress: We must build all relationship on a basis of understanding fellowship remembering the controlling principle that life on earth is meaningless apart from its eternal background. Growth of civilisation is marked by an increase of genuineness, sincerity and unselfishness. The only effective way of altering society is the hard and slow one of changing individuals. If we put first things first through patient effort and struggle, we will win power over circumstances and mould them. Only a humanity that strives after ethical and spiritual ideals can use the great triumphs of scientific knowledge for the true ends of civilisation.

The two volumes of *Indian Philosophy* demonstrate Radhakrishnan's forensic efficiency even when dealing with the profundities of our ancient compendiums of intellectual formulations and mystic realisations. He avoids vain argumentation and fruitless discussion. He scrupulously avoided splashing his scholarship by highlighting the differences that abound in India's philosophical systems. He was concerned with presenting a united front to the West and hence never tired of underlining the spiritual unity of the intellectually formulated metaphysical system.

Radhakrishnan sweetly lured the West to delve deeper into India's philosophy in order to re-formulate its own philosophical theories. He explained that philosophy itself was the extension of religious personality, and it is to such personalities that we must go in order to reap the full benefit of studying philosophy. He said, "The ideas of thinkers are evolved in the process of their life history. We must learn not only to reverence them but to acquire their spirit. The names of Vasishta and Visvamitra, Yajnavalkya and Gargi, Buddha and Mahavira, Gautama and Kanada, Kapila and Patanjali, Badarayana and Jaimini, Sankara and Ramanuja, are not merely themes for the historian but types of personality. With them philosophy is a world-view based on reflection and experience. Thought, when it thinks itself out to the end, becomes religion by being lived and tested by the supreme test of life. The discipline of philosophy is at the same time the fulfilment of a religious vocation".[26] An Idealist View of Life is his testament as a philosopher of our times.

Radhakrishnan's approach to philosophy was syncretic. His major contribution lay in his independent treatises. He was searching for a common bond, an underlying unity amidst the divisive philosophical disputations, amidst warfare and the gradual disintegration of creeds, sects and socio-politico order. He was looking for a synoptic vision, and he thought it was the business of philosophy to discover it. In *An Idealistic View of Life*, he distinguished three different senses of the word 'idea', from which the term 'idealism' has been derived. He acknowledged in the very first sentence that the term 'idealism' is decidedly ambiguous as it has been used to signify a variety of views. The word 'idea' usually stands for a mental image or a thought grasped within a mode of consciousness. The general thesis is that the observer is not gathering knowledge of the real world through these ideas, for ideas are more real and more immediate to the observer than the real world. Here, matter is downgraded. The view can also be called immaterialism. He thought there was an agreement in this respect between the Buddhist *Vijnana Vada* and some forms of British empiricism which reduce all knowledge to ideas in this sense. He wanted to emphasise a third sense of the word 'idea' that suited his philosophical motivation.

There is a second sense of the word 'idea' by which we can bring general 'notions' or, concepts, or even the categories of thought under its domain. By such categories of thought, Radhakrishnan said that the given, i.e. the 'uncategorised and unidealised' datum, reveals itself to the finite mind. He was not interested in the age-old realist-idealist controversy. So he moved forward to discuss the third sense of the word 'idea'.

The third sense of the word was indeed what Radhakrishnan wanted to derive at. This meaning lies behind such commonsense expressions as are sometimes made by an angry man: "Now, what is the big idea?" Apparently, the person has not understood something, some meaning or some purpose behind some act. This idea of 'idea' is what Radhakrishnan was after when he expounded his idealist view of life. It is very different from mentalism or the other forms of immaterialism. In fact the mentalism-materialism controversy does not have any relevance to this view of life. This idea is value or purpose. He said, "This idea of value is the operative creative force. An idealist view finds that the universe has meaning, has value. Ideal values are the dynamic forces, the driving power of the universe".[27]

In *An Idealist View of Life*, Radhakrishnan went to considerable length to not only contrast intellect and intuition but also to set up an elaborate defence of what he called intuitive knowledge over and above scientific knowledge. Here he claimed that there are at least three different ways of knowing. The distinction, according to him, is based upon the different ways by which each knowledge is produced. The first of these three ways of knowing is, of course, sense-experiences, which help us to know the features of the external world and thereby supply the data for natural science. The second is what he called logical knowledge, which is obtained by a process of analysis and synthesis. Both enable us to acquire control over the physical world. He was interested to argue in favour of the third avenue—intuition as the basis of knowledge.

Radhakrishnan produced a rare and forceful amalgam of the idealistic thought of Upanisadic origin and the ethics of action. The Upanisadic philosophy preached a way of life which could not be reconciled with the values related to man's mundane affairs. The skill of Radhakrishnan lies in constructing a system in which the absolute idealism running through the history of a Indian thought could be welded to Western activism with its theory of pure self and its contemporary welfare ethics: transcendentalism and practicalism telescoped into each other.

Through his writings, Radhakrishnan tried to establish the superiority of man's pure consciousness and man's concern about the ultimate destiny over his worldly and day to day engagements. Three major issues are reflected in his writings; the redefinition of the vision of the *Advaita Vedanta*, the relationship between *brahman* and the world, and the place of action in human life. These issues remain so intertwined in his thinking, that it is difficult to speak about any one of them in isolation. The basic programme of his writings is to present the classical Indian thought, as it is found in the *Upanishads*, the *Bhagavadgita* and the *Brahma Sutra*. He is one of those interpreters of the Indian tradition who take Indian philosophy and Indian religions as a unified thought system.

Radhakrishnan's theory of 'Reality and the World' emanated from his untainted dedication to the word of the *Advaita Vedanta*. His work consistently celebrate the original Upanisadic assumption that Reality is basically one, all-comprehensive, luminous and the source of multiple manifestations. *Brahman*, or the ultimate essence of all that exists, is for him the only frame of reference within which the world and the human existence in it could be understood. He markedly deviated from the central *Advaita Vedanta* assumption of *mayavada*, that is, that the phenomenal world in which man operates with various interests, desires, attachments, plans and so on, is illusory.

Radhakrishnan thought along firmly established Hindu lines, in the sense that despite the importance he attributed to worldly facts and, therefore, to science, technology and material civilisation, he was all the time convinced that the ultimate destiny of man lies in comprehending the spiritual force at the foundation of the emergence of the world. He criticised the West's one-sided development in scientific and technological enterprises, and its emphasis on the pursuit of comfort and luxury through emphasising the perennial values of the spirit taught in Hinduism. For him, the attainment of the Western style of life was not the ultimate ideal of man.[28] His role as an ambassador and as a special emissary of India to numerous countries was admirable—through this role he persuaded international gatherings to adopt broad-mindedness, a universality of outlook, and compassion for the poor and the suffering in the world. In its East-West synthesis, his philosophical output is noted for its integration of the West's endeavour to better the world through the application of science and technology.

REFERENCES

1. Parthasarathi, G. and Chattopadhyaya, D.P., *Radhakrishnan Centenary*, p. 42.
2. Radhakrishnan, S., *Fragments of a Confession*, p. 10.
3. *Ibid.*, p. 91.
4. Parthasarathi, G. and Chattopadhyaya, D.P., *op. cit.*, pp. 47-48.
5. *Ibid.*, p. 50.
6. Radhakrishnan, S., *An Idealist View of Life*, p. 28.
7. *Ibid.*, p. 33.
8. Radhakrishnan, S., *Contemporary Indian Philosophy*, p. 27.
9. Radhakrishnan, S., *The Hindu View of Life*, p. 18.
10. Parthasarathi, G., and Chattopadhyaya, D. P., *op. cit.*, p. 161.
11. Radhakrishnan, S., *Recovery of Faith*, p. 8.
12. Radhakrishnan, S., *Fragments of a Confession*, p. 24.
13. Radhakrishnan, S., *Reply to Critics*, p. 791.
14. Radhakrishnan, S., *Religion in a Changing World*, p. 79.
15. Radhakrishnan, S., *True Knowledge*, p. 77.
16. Clarissa Rodrigues, *The Social and Political Thought of Dr. S. Radhakrishnan*, pp. 16-17.
17. Radhakrishnan, S., *Occasional Speeches and Writings*, p. 200.
18. Radhakrishnan, S., *East and West*, p. 24.
19. Clarissa Rodrigues, *op. cit.*, pp. 18-21.
20. Radhakrishnan, S., *Recovery of Faith*, p. 73.
21. Radhakrishnan, S., *Religion and Society*, p. 47.
22. Radhakrishnan, S., *Eastern Religion and Western Thought*, p. 347.
23. Clarissa Rodrigues, *op. cit.*, pp. 25-26.
24. Radhakrishnan, S., *The Hindu View of Life*, p. 33.
25. Radhakrishnan, S., *Christian Social Thought in India*, p. 117.
26. Radhakrishnan, S., *Indian Philosophy*, Vol. 2, p. 78.
27. Radhakrishnan, S., *An Idealist View of Life*, p. 105.
28. Parthasarathi, G., and Chattopadhyaya, D.P., *op. cit.*, pp. 32-33.

4

ON HINDU DHARMA—I

The influence of Hinduism on Radhakrishnan's concept of Spiritual Religion is visible not only in the emphasis he gives to religion as a way of life and experience, but also in his stress on contemplation, tolerance, the basic equality of all religions and on religion being more a way of life than a form of thought. The other area of influence on Spiritual Religion is that Hinduism enjoins absolute liberty in thought but a strict code of practice. Radhakrishnan's views on Hindu *dharma* from *The Hindu View of Life* is reproduced here: Before we turn to the practical side of Hinduism, it is necessary to clear the ground by referring to some of the chief objections urged against the conception of Hindu ethics. The doctrine of *maya* is supposed to repudiate the reality of the world and thus make all ethical relations meaningless. The world of nature is said to be unreal and human history illusory. There is no meaning in time and no significance in life. To be delivered from this illusion which has somehow come to dominate the race of man is the end of all endeavour.

The Vedic thinkers adopted a realistic view of the world. In the *Upanishads* we have an insistence on the relative reality of the world. The illustrations of a musical instrument and its notes, the substances of clay and gold and the things made of clay and gold, make out that the objects of the world derive their being from the Supreme. As Yajnavalkya puts it, everything in the world is of value as leading to the realisation of self. When the *Svetasvatara Upanishad* looks upon the Supreme as the great *Mayin*, it suggests that this wonderful creation is his product. The *Upanishads* do not support the view at the supreme calls up appearances which have no existence except in deluded minds. The different theistic systems adopted by the large majority of the Hindus do not advocate the doctrine of *maya*. The theory is held by Samkara, who is regarded often as representing the standard type of

Hindu thought.

It is quite true that Samkara regards the world as *maya* and urges several reasons in support of his thesis. The manifold of experience whether of co-existence in space or sequence in time is ever incomplete and partial and we cannot unify it. There will always be a surplus uncovered by the largest unity. The fact that the time and space world cannot be rounded into a systematic whole indicates that it is imperfect and unreal. Again, the real must be exempt from all changes and persist for all time. The historical particulars do not persist for all time, they die every moment. We may interpret this idea in our own terms. The historical particular finishes its course when it reaches its end. If the end is not reached, if our lives are to be wasted in the pursuit of travelling perpetually and never arriving, then the world process is unmeaning and the cry that has gone forth that all is unity becomes justified. It cannot be interminable singing, there should also be such a thing as completion in a song. If the historical process is not all, if we are not perpetually doomed to the pursuit of an unattainable ideal, then we must reach perfection at some point of the historical process, and that will be the transcending of our historical individuality, of our escape from birth and death, or *samsara*. History is the working out of a purpose, and we are getting nearer and nearer to its fulfilment. *Moksha* is the realisation of the purpose of each individual. On the attainment of perfection the historical existence terminates. When one individual completes his purpose, he develops the universality of outlook characteristic of perfection, but retains his individuality as a centre of action. When the whole universe reaches its consummation, the liberated individuals lapse into the stillness of the Absolute. Those great forces which seem to be making silently and surely for the destruction of this starry universe in which our earth swims as a speck will reach their true destination. The world fulfils itself by self-destruction. Einstein's theory of relativity with its assumption that the spatio-temporal system is limited and measurable is not unfavourable to such a dissolution of the world. But this does not take away from the free being of God who is omnipotence or infinite possibility. The curtain will drop on this world, but another possibility, another plot, another drama may commence and go on for ages.

To some it may appear that such a collapse of the world is a poor termination to all our struggles, and so they picture to us an eternal heaven or even eternal hell, but the implication of these eternal states is one of eternal idleness. As Herbert Spencer put it, deviation from perfection or the perfect adjustment of the organism to the environment is decay. The state of perfection is a condition of absolute stillness, stagnation, death. There are thinkers, both in the East and the West, who look upon paradise as a state of activity where we sing the praises of God, and he has no end of patience in listening to his own glory. The only useful work which the liberated souls do is to help struggling humanity. So long as there are individuals who are unredeemed and so stand in need of saving knowledge, the liberated have some work to do. But if we allow that the world purpose is achieved, that all individuals have attained their perfection, there is nothing to be done. Aristotle says, 'Endless duration makes good no better, nor white any whiter". There is no creative process without travail, and the attainment of perfection for all means the end of creative activity. "Nothing that is perfectly real moves", according to Bradley. Activity is a characteristic of the historical process, and perfection is not historical. It lacks nothing and it cannot have any activity in it.

It is sometimes argued that the world process is infinite and so there will always be work to be done. In other words, there will never come a time when all individuals will reach their perfection. But this will be a frustration of the purpose of God. So long as the world process continues, the liberated souls retain their individualities, which they lose in the event of the liberation of all, or *sarvamukti.*

It is not fair to represent Samkara's view as illusionism. Samkara repudiates the subjectivism of *Vijnanavadins* and affirms the extra-mental reality of objects. His theory is not *drsti-srsti-vada,* that objects rise into being when we perceive them and disappear when we do not. We perceive objects and do not simply contemplate apparitions. Samkara distinguishes dreams from waking experiences and warns us against a confusion between the two. The experiences of waking life are not contradicted by anything else in our logical knowledge. He is a realist so far as our experience goes. Things control thought. Samkara's theory of *avidya* also confirms this view. For *avidya* is not a private profession of this or that individual mind; it is common to all minds, being the cosmic principle of finiteness. It is the cause of the whole empirical world (*Prthivyadiprapanca*) common to all (*Sarvasadharana*). *Moksha* or release of any one individual does not bring about the destruction of the world but only the displacement of a false outlook by a true one, *avidya* or *vidya.* When the illusion of the mirage is dissipated by scientific knowledge, the illusion stands there though it is no longer able to tempt us. The world is not so much denied as reinterpreted.

Samkara believes that the logical dualism between subject and object is not final. It rests on a monism. Subject and object are phases of spirit. They have no existence apart from *Brahman*. "There are in the world many universals with their particulars—both conscious and unconscious. All these universals in their graduated series are included and comprehended in one great universal, that is *Brahman* as a mass of intelligence". Samkara does not assert an identity between God and the world but only denies the independence of the world. As the Tikakara says : "The world is not identical with *Brahman*; only it has no separate being independent of its ultimate source". When Samkara denies the reality of effects, he qualifies his denial by some such phrase as 'independent of the cause' or 'independent of God'.

If we raise the question as to how the finite rises from out of the bosom of the infinite, Samkara says that it is an incomprehensible mystery, *maya*. We know that there is the absolute reality, we know that there is the empirical world, we know that the empirical world rests on the Absolute, but the how of it is beyond our knowledge. The hypothesis of creation is a weak one, and it assumes that God lived alone for some time and then suddenly it occurred to him to have company, when He put forth the world. The theory of manifestation is not more satisfying, for it is difficult to know how the finite can manifest the infinite. If we say that God is transformed into the world, the question arises whether it is the whole of God that is transformed or only a part. If it is the whole, then there is no God beyond the universe and we lapse into the lower pantheism. If it is only a part, then it means that God is capable of being partitioned. We cannot keep one part of God above and another part below. It would be like taking half a fowl for cooking, leaving the other half for laying eggs. Samkara believes that it is not possible to determine logically the relation between God and the world. He asks us to hold fast both ends. It does not matter if we are not able to find out where they meet.

The history of philosophy in India as well as Europe has been one long illustration of the inability of the human mind to solve the mystery of the relation to God to the world. The greatest thinkers are those who admit the mystery and comfort themselves by the idea that the human mind is not omniscient, Samkara in the East and Bradley in the West adopt this wise attitude of agnosticism. We have the universe with its distinctions. It is not self-sufficient. It rests on something else, and that is the Absolute. The relation between the two is a mystery. The idea expressed in the statement "And God saw everything that He had made and behold it was very good" and we have our doubts about it. Unable to believe that a good God could be responsible for the horrors of nature, Plato held that the goodness of God was made somewhat ineffective by the intractableness of nature which he tried in vain to control. The Gnostics strove to express the idea that God was trying to redeem a world created by the devil. Augustine from this worked out his view of 'total depravity' and the scheme of salvation. Some still clung to the idea of the omnipotence of God by paying him the doubtful compliment, as J.S. Mill says, of making him the creator of the devil. Leibniz argues that even if this world is in many ways defective, it is the best of all possible worlds; but this view implies an uncomplimentary reflection on the power of God. Hegelian absolutism is unable to account for the lapse of the perfect into the imperfect. Bergson emphasises the conflict of matter and life in the world and believes that the two are the negative and positive phases of one primal consciousness, but he is not able to account for the rise of the two tendencies from the first principle. Croce arrives at the different forms of spirit, theoretical and practical, but he does not give us any metaphysical deduction of these forms from the one spirit. If the forms are all, then there is no Absolute, and if there is no Absolute, it seems to be a sort of dissolute Absolute.

A wise agnosticism is more faithful to the situation. But the logical mind of man is not willing to admit defeat. It cannot rest in the idea that the Absolute is incomprehensible and that the world hangs on it somehow. It makes the Absolute determinate and relates the world to this determinate principle as its expression. In view of the weakness of the human mind Samkara allows these metaphors. The perfection of God overflows into the world. The world is the outflow of the surplus energies of God, the supreme artist. *Lila* or sport brings out the rationality, the freedom and the joyous exercise of spontaneity involved in the art of creation. We look upon God as a personal lord, and endow Him with the power of self-expression and self-communication. A sterile perfection is an inconceivability. The principle of self-expression is also called *maya*. It also stands for the principle of objectivity by interaction with which the subject self is able to express himself. But these attempts are devices to understand the nature of the relation of God to the world.

However that may by, no theory has ever asserted that life is a dream and all experienced events are illusions. One or two later followers of Samkara lend countenance to this hypothesis, but it cannot be regarded as representing the main tendency of Hindu thought.

The next objection goes to the opposite extreme. To the Hindu ethical rules are meaningless because the world is divine. Everything is God, and there is no excuse for our interfering with the sacred activities of the pickpocket and the perjurers. The critic believes that he refutes the theory of divine immanence associated with all forms of Indian thought when he exclaims, Is Piccadilly Circus God? is Hyde Park Corner God? The Hindu view rebels against the cold and formal conception of God who is external to the world, and altogether remote and transcendent. The natural law of the world is but a working of God's sovereign purpose. The uniformity of nature, the orderliness of the cosmos, and the steady reaching forward and upward of the course of evolution proclaim not the unconscious throbbing of a soulless engine, but the directing mind of an all-knowing spirit. The indwelling of God in the universe does not mean the identity of God with the universe. According to the latter view God is so immanent in everything that we have only to open our eyes to see God in it, but also there is nothing of God left outside the whole of things. God lies spread out before us. The world is not only a revelation, but an exhaustive revelation of God. Hindu thought takes care to emphasise the transcendent character of the Supreme. "He bears the world but is by no means lost in it". The world is in God and not God in the world. In the universe we have the separate existence of the individuals. Whether the divine spark burns dimly or brightly in the individual, the sparks are distinct from the central fire from which they issue.

Hindu thought admits that the immanence of God is a fact admitting of various degrees. While there is nothing which is not lit by God, God is more fully revealed in the organic than in the inorganic, more in the conscious than in the unconscious, more in man than in the lower creatures, more in the good man than in the evil. But even the worst of the world cannot be dismissed as completely undivine, fit only to be cast into hell fire. While Hinduism believes in the divine indwelling and declares that there is no escaping from the divine presence, it does not say that everything is God as we find it. Piccadilly is not God, though even Piccadilly cannot be unless it is allowed by divine activity. There are divine potentialities in even the worst of men, the ever lasting arms of God underneath the worst sinners. No one is really beyond hope. The worst sinner has a future even as the greatest saint has had a past. No one is so good or so bad as he imagines. The great souls of the world address themselves to the task of rousing the divine possibilities in the publicans and the sinners.

The doctrine of *Karma* is sometimes interpreted as implying a denial of human freedom, which is generally regarded as the basis of all ethical values. But when rightly viewed the law does not conflict with the reality of freedom. It is the principle of science which displaces belief in magic or the theory that we can manipulate the forces of the world at our pleasure. The course of nature is determined not by the passions and prejudices of personal spirits lurking behind it but by the operation of immutable laws. If the sun pursues his daily and the moon her nightly journey across the sky, if the silent procession of the seasons moves in light and shadow across the earth, it is because they are all guided in their courses by a power superior to them all. 'Verily O Gargi, at the command of that Imperishable, the sun and the moon stand apart, the earth and the sky stand apart . . . the moments, the hours, the days, the nights, the fortnights, the months, the seasons and the years stand apart. Verily O Gargi, at the command of that Imperishable, some rivers flow from the snowy mountains to the east, others to the west in whatever direction each flows. There is the march of necessity everywhere. The universe is lawful to the core.

The theory of *Karma* recognises the rule of law not only in outward nature, but also in the world of mind and morals. *Rta* manifests itself equally in nature and in human society. We are every moment making our characters and shaping our destinies. 'There is no loss of any activity which we commence nor is there any obstacle to its fulfilment. Even a little good that we may do will protect us against great odds'. What we have set our hearts on will not perish with this body. This fact inspires life with the present sense of eternity.

At a time when people were doing devil's work under divine sanction and consoling themselves by attributing everything to God's will, the principle of *Karma* insisted on the primacy of the ethical and identified God with the rule of law. All's law, yet all's God. *Karma* is not a mechanical principle but a spiritual necessity. It is the embodiment of the mind and will of God. God is its supervisor, *Karmadhyaksah*. Justice is an attribute of God. Character of God is represented by St. James as one "with whom can be no variation neither shadow that is cast by turning". Every act, every thought is weighed in the invisible but universal balance-scales of justice. The day of judgement is not in some remote future, but here and now, and none can escape it. Divine laws cannot be evaded. They are not so much imposed from without as wrought into our natures. Sin is not so much a defiance of God as a denial of soul, not so much a violation of law as a betrayal of self. We carry with as the whole of our past. It is an ineffaceable record which time cannot blur nor death erase.

There is room for repentance and consequent forgiveness on this scheme. The critic who urges that belief in *Karma* makes religious life, prayer and worship impossible has not a right understanding of it. In his opinion God has abdicated in favour of his law. To pray to God is as futile a superstition as to bid the storm give us strength, or the earthquake to forgive us our sins. Of course the Hindu does not look upon prayer as a sort of Aladdin's lamp to produce anything we want. God is not a magician stopping the sun in its course and staying the bullet in its march. But His truth and constancy, His mercy and justice find their embodiment in the implacable working of the moral law. Forgiveness is not a mitigation of God's justice but only an expression of it. We can insist with unflinching rigour on the inexorability of the moral law and yet believe in the forgiveness of sins. Spiritual growth and experience are governed by laws similar to those which rule the rest of the universe. If we sow to the flesh we shall of the flesh reap corruption. The punishment for a desecrated body is an enfeebled understanding and a darkened soul. If we deliberately fall into sin, shutting our eyes to moral and spiritual light, we may be sure that in God's world sin will find us out and our wilful blindness will land us in the ditch. A just God cannot refuse to any man that which he has earned. The past guilt cannot be wiped away by the atoning suffering of an outward substitute. Guilt cannot be transferred. It must be atoned for through the sorrow entailed by self-conquest. God cannot be bought over and sin cannot be glossed over.

The principle of *Karma* reckons with the material or the context in which each individual is born. While it regards the past as determined, it allows that the future is only conditioned. The spiritual element in man allows him freedom within the limits of his nature. Man is not a mere mechanism of instincts. The spirit in him can triumph over the automatic forces that try to enslave him. The *Bhagavadgita* asks us to raise the self by the self. We can use the material with which we are endowed to promote our ideals. The cards in the game of life are given to us. We do not select them. They are traced to our past *Karma*, but we can call as we please, lead what suit we win, and as we play, we gain or lose. And there is freedom.

What the individual will be cannot be predicted beforehand, though there is no caprice. We can predict an individual's acts so far as they are governed by habit, that is, to the extent his actions are mechanical and not affected by choice. But choice is not caprice. Free will in the sense of an undetermined, unrelated, uncaused factor in human action is not admitted, but such a will defies all analysis. It has nothing to do with the general stream of cause and effect. It operates in an irregular and chaotic way. If human actions are determined by such a will, there is no meaning in punishment or training of character. The theory of *Karma* allows man the freedom to use the material in the light of his knowledge. Man controls the uniformities in nature, his own mind and society. There is thus scope for genuine rational freedom, while indeterminism and chance lead to a false fatalism.

The universe is not one in which every detail is decreed. We do not have a mere unfolding of a pre-arranged plan. There is no such thing as absolute prescience on the part of God, for we are all his fellow-workers. God is not somewhere above us and beyond us, He is also in us. The divine in us can, if utilised, bring about even sudden conversions. Evolution in the sense of epigenesis is not impossible. For the real is an active developing life and not a mechanical routine.

The law of *Karma* encourages the sinner that it is never too late to mend. It does not shut the gates of hope against despair and suffering, guilt and peril. It persuades us to adopt a charitable view towards the sinner, for men are more often weak than vicious. It is not true that the heart of man is desperately wicked and that he prefers evil to good, the easy descent to hell and to the steep ascent to heaven.

Unfortunately, the theory of *Karma* became confused with fatality in India when man himself grew feeble and was disinclined to do his best. It was made into an excuse for inertia and timidity and was turned into a message of despair and not of hope. It said to the sinner, 'Not only are you a wreck, but that is all you ever could have been. That was your preordained being from the beginning of time'. But such a philosophy of despair is by no means the necessary outcome of the doctrine of *Karma*.

Let us now turn to the practical side of Hinduism. Hinduism is more a way of life than a form of thought. While it gives absolute liberty in the world of thought it enjoins a strict code of practice. The theist and the atheist, the sceptic and the agnostic may all be Hindus if they accept the Hindu system of culture and life. Hinduism insists not on religious conformity but on a spiritual and ethical outlook in life. "The performer of the good—and not the believer in this or that view—can never get into an evil state. In a very real sense practice precedes theory." Only by doing the will does one know the doctrine. Whatever our theological beliefs and metaphysical opinions may be, we ore all agreed that we should be kind and honest, grateful to our benefactors and sympathetic to the unfortunate. Hinduism insists on a moral life and draws into fellowship all who feel themselves bound to the claims which the moral law makes upon them. Hinduism is not a sect but a fellowship of all who accept the law of right and earnestly seek for the truth.

Dharma is right action. In the *Rig Veda, rita* is the right order of the universe. It stands for both the *satya* or the truth of things as well as the *dharma* or the law of evolution. *Dharma* formed from the root *dhir*, to hold means that which holds a thing and maintains it in being. Every form of life, every group of men has its *dharma*, which is the law of its being. *Dharma* or virtue is conformity with the truth of things; *adharma* or vice is opposition to it. Moral evil is disharmony with the truth which encompasses and controls the world.

Desires constitute the springs of human action: The life of man centres round certain basic cravings, each distinct from the other in its object and each stimulating men to a particular mode of activity in order to satisfy it. If the several desires were independent of one another and never crossed or modified one another, then their different expressions would be separate and uncoordinated. Family life will have little to do with economic pursuits. Industrial relations will be ethically colourless. Religious activities may be indifferent to the secular sides of life. But man is a whole, and so all his activities have an overarching unity. Each individual has in him the sex and the parental instincts, love of power and wealth, desire for the common good and a hunger for communion with the unseen. These different activities react upon and modify one another. They function in interdependence in man's life. If life is one, then there is one master science of life which recognises the four supreme ends of *dharma* or righteousness, *artha* or wealth, *kama* or artistic and cultural life, and *moksa* or spiritual freedom. The Hindu code of practice links up the realm of desires with the perspective of the eternal. It binds together the kingdoms of earth and heaven.

Hinduism does not believe in any permanent feud between the human world of natural desires and social aims and the spiritual life with its discipline and aspiration on the other. It condemns only natural existence which is unrelated to the background. Such a life which concentrates on this world and its good things is not satisfying, for the greatest prosperity comes to its end, dissolving into emptiness. The world and all else on which we pin our faith will desert us in the moment of our triumph. The Hindu thinker dwells on the evanescence of the world and its pitiful futility if its connection with the eternal is snapped.

All worldly relationships have their and, but they cannot be ignored. To behave as if they do not exist simply because they do not persist is to court disaster. The external is manifested in the temporal, and the latter is the pathway to the former. Truth in the finite aspect leads us to infinite truth. Renunciation is the feeling of detachment from the finite as finite and attachment to the finite as the embodiment of the infinite. The two are bound to each other and to separate them is ruinous. The *Upanisad* says: "In darkness are they who worship only the world, but in greater darkness they who worship the infinite alone. He who accepts both saves himself from death by the knowledge of the former and attains immortality by the knowledge of the latter".

Artha takes note of the economic and the political life of man, the craving for power and property. The urge which gives rise to property is something fundamental in human nature. Unless we change the constitution of the human mind, we cannot eradicate the idea of property. For most men property is the medium for the expression of personality and intercourse with others.

While the pursuit of wealth and happiness is a legitimate human aspiration, they should be gained in ways of righteousness (*dharma*), if they are to lead ultimately to the spiritual freedom of man (*moksha*). Each one of these ends requires ethical discipline. Freedom can be obtained only through bonds of discipline and surrender of personal inclination. To secure the freedom to acquire and to enjoy we have to limit ourselves and bind our will in certain ways. The countries which are politically free and largely bound in thought and practice. Political freedom is not possible without a large curtailment of freedom of thought and action. In the interests of spiritual freedom Hindu society regulated the most intimate details of daily life, and they are the rules of *dharma*. These rules are not the same in all parts of the country or in all periods of Hindu history. The Hindu legislators accepted the bewildering variety of customs professed by the tribes in India as the civilisation spread from the Indus to the Cape. The law books recognise the variety, though they try to refine whatever seems to be morally objectionable. While recognising them all an ideal standard is enjoined which interceptibly brings about a refinement of the customs. According to the *Taittirya Upanishad*, the youngman is asked in cases of doubt to take as his authority what is done in similar circumstances by the Brahmins "competent to judge, apt and devoted but not harsh, lovers of virtue". Manu urges that the conduct of good people and righteous souls of the regenerate classes may be regarded as consistent with the customs of all countries, families and castes.

Moksha is spiritual realisation. The Hindu *Dharma* says, man does not live by bread alone, nor by his work, capital, ambition or power or relations to external nature. He lives or must live by his life of spirit. *Moksha* is self-emancipation, the fulfilment of the spirit in us in the heart of the eternal. This is what gives ultimate satisfaction, and all other activities are directed to the realisation of this end.

As to the methods of obtaining freedom, the Hindu thinker adopted a very catholic attitude. "As the birds fly in the air, as the fish swim in the sea, leaving no traces behind, even so is the pathway to God traversed by the seeker of spirit".

The different pathways have been broadly distinguished into the three types of *jnana* or wisdom, *bhakti* or devotion and *karma* or service. The three are not exclusive, but emphasise the dominant aspects. Wisdom does not mean intellectual acumen or dialectical power. *Jnana* is realised experience. We are saved from sin only when we live in the presence of God. If we have true insight, right action will take care of itself. Truth cannot but act rightly. The way of devotion is the most popular one. Sinners as well as saints, ignorant as well as learned, foolish as well as wise find it easy. Prayer and petition, fasting and sacrifice, communion and self-examination, all are included in the life of devotion. In its highest flights, *bhakti* coincides with *jnana*, and both these issues in right *karma* or virtuous life.

While the individual and the social sides of *karma* are inseparably intertwined, the theory of *varna* or caste emphasises the social aspect, and that of *ashrama* or stages of life the individual aspect. The four stages of *brahmacharya* or the period of training, *grahastya* or the period of work for the world as a householder, *vanaprastha* or the period of retreat for the loosening of the social bonds, and *sannyasa* or the period of renunciation and expectant awaiting of freedom indicate that life is a pilgrimage to the eternal life through different stages.

The first period is that of training and discipline of body and mind. Plastic youth is moulded to a life of duty. The student is required to live for a fixed period in the house of his teacher, where he is taught the arts and sciences which would be useful to him in after life. Women were also entitled to *brahmacharya*. They were given the training of their classes, and thus enabled to take up the functions of the caste in the emergencies of life. Restrictions regarding Vedic study were introduced when women of other racial stocks with different customs were accepted in marriage.

The second stage is that of the householder or the *grahastha.* A human being is not ordinarily self-sufficing. The God of Aristotle may enjoy his solitary existence, but not the men and women of the world. These are as rule encouraged to enter the married life. India has known for centuries what Freud is popularising in Europe, that repressed desires are more corrupting in their effects than those exercised openly and freely. Monastic tendencies were discouraged until one had a normal expression for natural impulses. He who runs back from marriage is in the same boat with one who runs away from battle. Only failures in life avoid occasions for virtue. Marriage is regarded as sacred. The very gods are married. When the Hindu descends from the adoration of the absolute and takes to the worship of a personal god, his god has always a consort. He does not worship a bachelor or a virgin. Siva is *arthanarisvara*, and his image signifies the cooperative interdependent, separately incomplete but jointly complete masculine and feminine functions of the supreme being. There is nothing unwholesome or guilty about the sex life. Through the institution of marriage it is made the basis of intellectual and moral intimacies. Marriage is not so much a concession to human weakness as a means of spiritual growth. It is prescribed for the sake of the development of personality as well as the continuance of the family ideal. Marriage has this social side. Every family is a partnership between the living and the dead. The *Sraddha* ceremony is intended to impress the idea of the family solidarity on the members. At the end of the cerèmony the performer asks, "Let me, O fathers ! Have a hero for a son".

The Hindu ideal emphasises the individual and the social aspects of the institution of marriage. Man is not a tyrant nor is woman a slave, but both are servants of a higher ideal to which their individual inclinations are to be subordinated. Sensual love is sublimated into self-forgetful devotion . Marriage for the Hindu is a problem and not a datum. Except in the pages of fiction we do not have a pair agreeing with each other in everything, tastes and temper, ideals and interests. Irreducible peculiarities there will always be, and the task of the institution of marriage is to use these differences to promote a harmonious life. Instincts and passions are the raw material which are to be worked up into an ideal whole. Though there is some choice with regards to our mates, there is a large element of chance in the best of marriages. Carve as we will that mysterious block of which our life is made, the black vein of destiny or chance, whatever we may call it, appears again and again in it. That marriage is successful which transforms a chance mate into a life companion. Marriage is not the end of the struggle, it is but the beginning of a strenuous life where we attempt to realise a larger ideal by subordinating our private interests and inclinations. Service of a common ideal can bind together the most unlike individuals. Love demands its sacrifices. By restraint and endurance, we raise love to the likeness of the divine.

In an ideal marriage the genuine interests of the two members are perfectly reconciled. The perfectly ethical marriage is the monogamous one. The relation of Rama and Sita, or Savitri and Satyavan, where the two stand by each other against the whole world, is idealised in the Hindu scriptures. In the absence of absolute perfection we have to be content with approximations. We need not, however, confound the higher with the lower. Eight different kinds of marriages are recognised in the Hindu law books. Manu did not shut his eyes to the practices of his contemporaries. He arranges the different kinds of marriages in an order. While marriages in which personal inclination is subordinated rank high, those by mutual choice, force, purchase come lower. The lowest is *paisaca*. When the lover ravishes a maiden without her consent, when she is asleep, or intoxicated or deranged in mind, we have a case of *paisaca* marriage. It is a very low kind of marriage, but admitted as valid with the laudable motives of giving the injured women the status of wives and their offspring legitimacy.

Insistence on the interests of the family led to a compromise of the monogamous ideal. While the monogamous ideal is held up as the best, polygamy was also tolerated. When you have on male offspring, or when, by mistake or chance, you seduce a woman when you are married, it is your duty to protect her from desertion and from public scorn, save her from a life of infamy and degradation, and protect her children who are in no way responsible for the ways of their parents; in such cases polygamy is permissible. The story of the epic *Ramayana* has for one of its chief lessons the evils of polygamy. The palace of Dasaratha was a centre of intrigue, and Rama, the hero of the story, stands up for the monogamous ideal.

A system which looks upon marriage as compulsory for all has its own weaknesses, though it does not develop large numbers of unmarried women who see no meaning in life. It is obliged to discountenance the remarriage of widows. It unconsciously tends to lower the marriageable age of girls. It is necessary for the leaders to remember the Hindu ideals and bring about a more satisfactory state of affairs.

The recognition of the spiritual ideal of marriage requires us to regard the marriage relation as an indissoluble one. So long as we take a small view of life and adopt for our guide the fancy or feeling of the moment, marriage relation cannot be regarded as permanent. In the first moments of infatuation we look upon our partners as angels from heaven, but soon the wonder wears away, and if we persist in our passion for perfection, we become agitated and often bitter. The unrest is the effect of a false ideal. The perfect relation is to be created and not found. The existence of incompatibility is a challenge to a more vigorous effort. To resort to divorce is to confess defeat. The misfits and the maladjustments are but failures.

Modern conditions are responsible for the large numbers of divorces and separations. Life has become too hurried. We have no time to understand one another. To justify our conduct, we are setting up exaggerated claims on behalf of the individual will and are strongly protesting against discipline. We are confusing self-expression and self-development with a life of instincts and passions. We tend to look upon ourselves as healthy animals and not spiritual beings. We have had sin with us from the beginning of our history, but we have recently begun to worship it. It is not very modern for a man or woman who is sick of his or her partner to take to another, but what is really modern is the new philosophy in justification of it. Disguised feeling is masquerading as advanced thought. The woman who gives up her husband for another is idealised as a heroine who has had the courage to give up the hypocritical moral codes and false sentiments, while she who clings to her husband through good report and bad is a cowardly victim of conventions. Sex irregularities are becoming less shocking and more popular.

Though we have had our share of exaggerating the wickedness of women, and though we have some texts which regard the woman as the eternal temptress of the man Adam, a snare of perdition, as Donaldson expressed it, "a fireship continually striving to get alongside the male man-of-war and blow him up into pieces", the general Hindu view of woman is an exalted one. It regards the woman as the helpmate of man in all his work, *Sahadharmini*. The Hindu believes in the speciality of the contribution which woman makes to the world. She has special responsibilities and special duties. Even such an advanced thinker as Mrs. Bertrand Russell allows that 'each class and sex has that to give to the common stock of achievement, knowledge and thought which it alone can give, and robs itself and the community by inferior imitation. So long as children cannot be shaken from heaven, but have to be built within their mothers' bodies, so long will there be a specific function for women. As the bearing and rearing of children take a good deal of their time and attention, women were relieved of the economic responsibilities for the family. While man is expected to take to the worldly pursuits, woman is capable of great heights of self-control and self-denial. The stricter code of morality applied to woman is really a compliment to them, for it accepts the natural superiority of the women. But the modern woman, if I may say so, is losing her self-respect. She does not respect her own individuality and uniqueness, but is paying an unconscious tribute to man by trying to imitate him. She is fast becoming masculine and mechanical. Adventurous pursuits are leading her into conflict with her own inner nature.

The third stage arises when the responsibilities of home are given up. The wife accompanies the husband to the forest, if she shares his spiritual aims. According to Manu, one must enter the third stage when one becomes a grandfather, or one's skin begins to show wrinkles or one's hair turns grey. When one's bodily powers wane, it is time to depart to the forest and prepare oneself for the true life of the spirit. The main objective of this stage is to escape from the bustle of life into the solitude of the forest to meditate on the higher problems.

The stature of man is not to be reduced to the requirements of the society. Man is much more than the custodian of its culture or protector of his country or producer of its wealth. His social efficiency is not the measure of his spiritual manhood. The soul which is our spiritual life contains our infinity within it. What shall it profit a man if he gains the whole world but loses his own soul? A Sanskrit verse reads: "For the family sacrifice the individual; for the community the family; for the country the community, and for the soul the whole world". Family and country, nation and the world cannot satisfy the soul in man. Each individual is called upon at a certain stage of his life to give up his wife and children and his caste and work. The last part of life's road has to be walked in single file.

The aim of the *sannyasin* is not to free himself from the cares of outward life, but to attain a state of spiritual freedom when he is not tempted by riches or honour, and is not elated by success or depressed by failure. He develops a spirit of equanimity and so "bears patiently improper words and does not insult anyone; he does not hate anyone for the sake of his physical body". These free men are solitary souls who have not any personal attachments or private ambitions, but embody in their own spirit the freedom of the world. They take on the wideness of the whole earth, dwell in love and walk in righteousness. The social order regards the *sannyasin* as a parasite since he does not contribute to it materially and does not care for its forms. The state looks on him with suspicion as he does not profess any loyalty to any family or church, race or nation. He does not function in any industrial factory, social system or political machine. These *sannyasins* do not serve our policies that make the world unsafe for human life, do not promote our industries that mechanise persons, and do not support our national egoisms that provoke wars. Patriotism is not enough for these fine souls. Life, and not India's life or England's life, demands their devotion. They look upon all men and all groups as equal.

While some forms of Christianity and Buddhism judge the life of the world to be inferior to the life of the monk, and would have loved to place the whole of mankind at one swoop in the cloister, Hinduism while appreciating the life of the *sannyasin* refrained from condemning the state of the householder. Every state is necessary, and insofar as it is necessary it is good. The blossom does not deny the leaf and the leaf does not deny the stalk nor the stalk the root. The general rule is that we should pass from stage to stage gradually.

The liberated soul is not indifferent to the welfare of the world. Renunciation is the surrendering of the notions of I and mine, and not the giving up of the work enjoined by the scriptures. It is related of the Buddha that when he was on the threshold of *nirvana* he turned away and took the vow never to cross it so long as a single being remained subject to sorrow and suffering. The same idea comes out in the sublime verse of the *Bhagavata*: "I desire not the supreme state (of bliss) with its eight perfections, nor the cessation of rebirth. May I take up the sorrow of all creatures who suffer and enter into them so that they may be made free from grief". Mahadeva the prince of ascetics drank poison for the sake of the world. Freedom on the highest level of existence expresses itself on the lower as courage to suffer, sacrifice, and die.

This fourfold plan of life yet dominates the Hindu mind. The general character of a society is not always best expressed by the mass of its members. There exists in every community a natural elite, which better than all the rest represents the soul of the entire people, its great ideals, its strong emotions and its essential tendency. The whole community looks to them as their example. When the wick is ablaze at its tip, the whole lamp is said to be burning.

5

ON HINDU DHARMA—II

Radhakrishnan thought that the caste system promoted individuality which consists in the willing acceptance of obligations. But the individual is not offered a choice since caste is dependent on birth. In his assessment of the caste system, Radhakrishnan has shown how an account of the tolerant spirit of Hinduism, the caste system achieved an assimilation and civilising of various races. In its absence there would have been a greater number of depressed classes. He thought that the caste provided man with the opportunity to express his nature and to serve society. His views on Hindu *dharma* from *The Hindu View of Life* is reproduced here:

The institution of caste illustrates the spirit of comprehensive synthesis characteristic of the Hindu mind with its faith in the collaboration of races and the cooperation of cultures. Paradoxical as it may seem, the system of caste is the outcome of tolerance and trust. Though it has now degenerated into an instrument of oppression and intolerance, though it tends to perpetuate inequality and develop the spirit of exclusiveness, these unfortunate effects are not the central motives of the system. If the progressive thinkers of India had the power, as they undoubtedly have the authority, they would transform the institution out of recognition. It is not the evils of the system that I am here concerned with so much as the underlying principles.

Any survey of the castes of the present day will reveal the complex origin of the institution. Castes are of many kinds, tribal, racial, sectarian, occupational. Some are due to migration. When members of an old caste migrate to a different part of the country, they become a new caste.

As it is clear from the Sanskrit word *varna*, caste had originally reference to colour. If we look into the past history of India, we see how the country has been subjected to one race invasion after another.

Even at the beginning of her history India was peopled by various racial groups, the dark aboriginal tribes, the sturdy Dravidians, the yellow-skinned Mongols and the blithe, forceful Aryans. Very soon she developed intimate intercourse with the Persians, the Greeks and the Scythians, and some of these settled down in India. No other country in the world has had such racial problems as India.

Regarding the solution of the problem of racial conflicts the different alternatives which present themselves are those of extermination, subordination, identification or harmonisation. The first course has been adopted often in the course of the history of the world. The trail of man is dotted with the graves of countless communities which reached an untimely end. But is there any justification for this violation of human life? Have we any idea of what the world loses when one racial culture is extinguished? It is true that the Red Indians have not made, to all appearance, any contribution to the world's progress, but have we any clear understanding of their undeveloped possibilities which, in God's good time, might have come to fruition? Do we know so much of ourselves and the world and God's purpose as to believe that our civilisation, our institutions and our customs are so immeasurably superior to those of others, not only what others actually possess but what exists in them potentially? We cannot measure beforehand the possibilities of a race. Civilisations are not made in a day, and had the fates been kindlier and we less arrogant in our ignorance, the world, I dare say, would have been richer for the contributions of the Red Indians. Our civilisation is quite recent when compared with the antiquity of man and the differentiation of human types. Some of the ancestors of the Great British people who are now in the vanguard of humanity were not much advanced as depicted by Julius Caesar. Who could understand the great potentialities of the savages of Britain dressed in skins at their religious worship burning men alive to appease their gods? No one acquainted with the ancestors of the Teutons would have anticipated for them their glorious contributions to music and metaphysics. Human potentiality is so great, and our knowledge of fundamental racial differences so little, that the cruel repression and extermination of races is not the part of wisdom. A little understanding of human nature and history will enable us to sympathise with the savage and the primitive, the barbarous and the backward, and help us to see that they also in their imperfect fashions are struggling towards that abiding city which shines in dazzling splendour up the steep and narrow way. Every people, every tribe however little advanced in its stage of development, represents a certain psychic type or pattern. The interests of humanity require that every type should be assisted and educated to its adequate expression and development. No race lives to itself and no race dies to itself. Besides, the backwardness of races is due to environmental conditions, physical, social and cultural. Races show considerable powers of adaptation when an external stimulus is applied to them.

When extermination is impossible, the powerful races of the world adopt the second alternative of subordination. They act on the maxim, spare the slave and smash the rebel. The superior races of the world cannot have a clean conscience if they remember their dealings with the coloured ones on the Congo in Brazil, in Peking at the time of the Boxer revolution, and in America today. For a man like Lord Milner the British Empire meant the brotherhood of communities of like blood and the mastery of the British race over the non-British dependencies. Civilisation is not the suppression of races less capable of or less advanced in culture by people of higher standing. God does not give us the right to destroy or enslave the weak and the unfit. One race may not be as clever or as strong as another, and yet the highest idealism requires that we should give equality of opportunity even to unequal groups. We must respect the independence of every people and lead the backward ones to a full utilisation of the opportunities of their environment and a development of their distinctive natural characteristics.

Racial fusion on a large scale is an impossibility, if it is to be achieved in a short period of time. For long centuries of social tradition and natural inheritance have produced marked divergencies of temperament, mentality and physique which cannot be destroyed at a stroke. Nor is it necessary to do away with race individualities and differences to solve the race problem. Uniformity is not the meaning of unity.

In dealing with the problem of the conflict of the different racial groups, Hinduism adopted the only safe course of democracy, viz. that each racial group should be allowed to develop the best in it without impeding the progress of others. Every historical group is unique and specific and has an ultimate value, and the highest morality requires that we should respect its individuality. Caste, on its racial side, is the affirmation of the infinite diversity of human groups. Though the Vedic Aryans started their life in India with a rigid and narrow outlook, regarding themselves as a sort of chosen people, they soon became universal in intention and developed an ethical code applicable to the whole of humanity, a *manava dharma*. Those who tried to bring together different races in India are worshipped as the makers of the Hindu society. Rama used the aboriginal tribes in the work of civilising the South. He brought together the Aryans and the non-Aryans, and so did Krishna and the Buddha.

When the aboriginal tribes and others accepted the Hindu standpoint they did not surrender their own individuality but modified it as well as the Hindu spirit which they absorbed. The change isasmuch in the new group form as in the old ideal. The tribes were admitted into the larger life of Hinduism with the opportunities and the responsibilities which that life gave them, the opportunities to share in the intellectual and cultural life of the Hindus and the responsibilities of contributing to its thoughts, its moral advancement and its spiritual worth—in short, to all that makes a nation's life. Each group dealt with the Hindu ideas in its own characteristic way. We need not overrate the stagnation of the aboriginal tribes. They were also raised above the welter of savagery and imbued with the spirit of gentleness. Sheltered on the same soil, bound together by common interests, evolving under the influence of common psychic and moral surroundings, the different component tribes not only improved in their level but become adapted to each other in spite of diversity of origin. Mr. Valentine Chirol remarks: "The supple and subtle force of Hinduism has already in prehistoric times welded together the discordant beliefs and customs of a vast variety of races into a comprehensive fabric sufficiently elastic to shelter most of the indigenous populations of India, and sufficiently rigid to secure the Aryan Hindu ascendancy".

Indiscriminate racial amalgamation was not encouraged by the Hindu thinkers. The Hindu scriptures recognised the rules about food and marriage which the different communities were practising. What we regard as the lower castes have their own taboos and customs, laws and beliefs which they have created for themselves in the course of ages. Every member of the group enters into the possession of the inheritance bequeathed. It is the law of use and won't that distinguishes one group from its neighbours. Caste is really custom. Crude and false as the customs and beliefs of others may seem to us, we cannot deny that they help the community adopting them to live at peace itself and in harmony with others. It is a point of social honour for every member to marry within his own caste, and a 'low' caste woman would refuse to marry one outside her caste, even if he were from a 'higher' one.

Though the Hindu theory of caste does not favour the indiscriminate crossing of men and women, interbreeding has been practised, largely unconsciously, and the essential differences of tribes were modified. Purely anthropological groups are found only among primitive and savage peoples, and not in the societies which play a part in the march of humanity. There has been a general infusion of foreign blood into the Hindu race, and within the race itself there has been a steady flow of blood from the Brahmin to the Candala. The inter-mixture of blood has been carefully regulated by means of *anuloma* and *pratiloma* marriages, though the tendency to indiscriminate crossing was not encouraged. While Manu recommends marriages of members of the same caste he tolerates marriages of men with women of the 'lower castes'. Though he does not justify *pratiloma* marriages, i.e. marriages of women of the 'higher' castes with men of the 'lower', he describes the various progeny of such marriages. While they were not regarded as proper there is no doubt that they prevailed. Castes of a mixed type have been formed in order to regularise the position of groups originally proceeding from marriages forbidden or discountenanced by custom or law but condoned after a time. Some of the groups which are today regarded as 'untouchable' are said to have arisen by indiscriminate crossing.

While we are dealing with this question, it may be observed that the Hindu system did not condemn all crossing as mischievous. When the stocks are of nearly the same level, crossing is highly beneficial. The deplorable example of the Eurasians is frequently quoted, but then the two stocks happen to be widely different. Besides, the circumstances which accompany their birth and training will damage the best of men. The white man who seduces an Indian nearly always abandons her when she becomes a mother, and the child coming into the world as the product of irregular mating, badly nourished and much despised, grows up generally in conditions which are not very desirable. Not only inheritance but environment also counts.

Yet the principle of *savarna* marriages is not unsound. It is a difficult question to decide whether the influence of heredity is so great as to justify *savarna* marriages only. The question of nature versus nurture is still hotly debated. Democrats are quite certain that it is not blue blood or inherited traits that make for the superiority of the upper classes. The Hindu view, however, has the support of ancient Greek thought and modern science. The Greeks believed in heredity and actually developed a theory of race betterment by the weeding out of inferior strains and the multiplication of the superior ones. As early as the sixth century B. C. the Greek poet Theognis of Megara wrote, "We look for rams and asses and stallions of good stock, and one believes that good will come from good; yet a good man minds not to wed the evil daughter of an evil sire . . . Marvel not that stock of our folk is tarnished, for the good is mingling with the base". We are all familiar with Plato's views of biological selection as the best method of race improvement. Aristotle also believed that the state should encourage the increase of superior types. There has been during the eighteenth century an increasing insistence on the natural equality of men. Adopting the views of Locke and Rousseau, the thinkers of French and American declarations on human rights, Buckle held that men were moulded by their environments as so much soft clay. Modern science, however, holds that this view exaggerates the influence of the environment. Progress does not depend on a mere change of surroundings. Darwin's teaching that evolution proceeds by heredity was taken up by Galton and other biologists like Weismann and De Vries, and the science of eugenics rests today on somewhat safe and sound foundations. The marvellous potency of the germ-plasm is shown by carefully isolating and protecting it against external influences when it steadily follows its predetermined course. Even when interfered with, it tends to overcome the opposition and resume its normal course. Every cell of our body contains tiny chromosomes, which practically determine our being, height and weight, form and colour, nervous organisation and vital energy, temperament and intelligence. Half the number of chromosomes in every cell of our body comes from the father and half from the mother, and they transmit to us most faithfully the qualities of our parents. Any stupidity or insanity of our parents, grand-parents or great-grand-parents will be transmitted to our children and our children's children. The Hindu thinkers, perhaps through a lucky intuition or an empirical generalisation, assumed the fact of heredity and encouraged marriages among those who are of approximately the same type and quality. If a member of a first-class family marries another of poor antecedents the good inheritance of the one is debased by the bad inheritance of the other, with the result that the child starts life with a heavy handicap. If the parents are about the same class the child would be practically the equal of the parents. Blood tells. We cannot make genius out of mediocrity or good ability out of inborn stupidity by all the aids of the environment.

It does not, however, mean that nature is all and nurture is nothing.

The kind of nurture depends on the group and its type. So long as we had the caste system, both nature and nurture cooperated. There is such a thing as social heredity. Each successive generation acquires by conscious effort the social acquisitions of the groups.

If we want to prevent the suicide of the social order, some restrictions have to be observed with regard to marital relations. Marriages should be, not necessarily in one's own caste but among members of approximately the same level of culture and social development. For castes also degenerate. As sons are expected to follow the calling of their fathers, superior individuals are not allowed to grow higher than the groups, and the inferior ones are not allowed to sink lower into their proper scale. Caste, as it is, has not made room for high-born incompetents and low-born talents. While every attempt should be made to energise the weak and the lowly by education and moral suasion, indiscriminate marriage relations do not seem to be always desirable.

Without creating great racial disturbances the Hindu spirit brought about a gradual racial harmony. The synthesis of caste started as a social organisation of different ethnic types. There is no doubt that there are many animists who have not been assimilated by Hinduism. When Hindu India lost its independence its work of assimilation and reform stopped, though the present day Hindu leaders are slowly realising their responsibilities towards them.

Caste was the answer of Hinduism to the forces pressing on it from outside. It was the instrument by which Hinduism civilised the different tribes it took in. Any group of people appearing exclusive in any sense is a caste. Whenever a group represents a type a caste arises. If a heresy is born in the bosom of the mother faith and if it spreads and produces a new type, a new caste arises. The Hindu Society has differentiated as many types as can be reasonably differentiated, and is prepared to accept new ones as they arise. It stands for the ordered complexity, the harmonised multiplicity, the many in one which is the clue to the structure of the universe.

Today many brilliant writers are warning us of a world-conflict of races. The rise of racial self consciousness is a peculiar phenomenon of our times. The coloured peoples are clamouring rightly for a share in the control of the world. Those who are politically subject are demanding political freedom. The conflict between emigration and immigration countries is highly acute. When the weak, the ignorant and the slothful races were wiped out or subordinated, it was argued in defence of this method that the savage races and the primitive peoples could not expect to remain undisturbed in their habitat, for the world cannot afford to let fields lie fallow and ore remain undug, and if the chance occupants of resourceful areas are too feeble and sluggish to develop them, their displacement by people who can redeem the waste places is necessary and right. The mere fact that in the chance wanderings of the race, a particular Tribe happened to pitch its tent on a diamond field or an oil-well whose existence it had not guessed and whose use it had not understood, does not give that tribe an exclusive claim to its possession. No country belongs to itself. The needs of the world are the paramount consideration. But this argument in not applied to the present conditions. While the pressure of population draws masses of men from their countries to seek employment elsewhere, and while there are immense underpopulated areas requiring intelligent labour for the development of their resources, the adjustments are not allowed to take place. America, Australia, South Africa, etc., are forbidden lands to the coloured people. Latin America is very sparsely populated, and might easily contain ten times its present number and increase its production to an almost unlimited extent. There are Territories which thirst for population and others which are overflowing with it, and yet pride of race and love of power are overriding all considerations of abstract justice and economic necessity. It is not my purpose here to deal with the practical difficulties in the way of an easy solution of the racial problem. They are great, but they can be solved only by the consciousness of the earth as one great family and an endeavour to express this reality in all our relationships. We must work for a world in which all races can blend and mingle, each retaining its special characteristics and developing whatever is best in it.

Very early in the history of Hinduism, the caste distinctions came to mean the various stratifications into which the Hindu society settled. The confusion between the tribal and the occupational is the cause of the perpetuation of the old exclusiveness of the tribal customs in the still stringent rules which govern the constitution of each caste. Caste on its social side is a product of human organisation and not a mystery of divine appointment. It is an attempt to regulate society with a view to actual differences and ideal unity. The first reference to it is in the *Purusa Sukta*, where the different sections of society are regarded as the limbs of the great self. Human society is an organic whole, the parts of which are naturally dependent in such a way that each part in fulfilling its distinctive function conditions the fulfilment of function by the rest, and is in turn conditioned by the fulfilment of its function by the rest. In this sense the whole is present in each part, while each part is indispensable to the whole. Every society consists of groups working for the fulfilment of the wants of the society. As the different groups work for a common end they are bound by a sense of unity and social brotherhood. The cultural and the spiritual, the military and the political, the economic classes and the unskilled workers constitute the four-bold caste organisation. The different functions of the human life were clearly separated and their specific and complementary character was recognised. Each caste has its social purpose and function, its own code and tradition. It is a close corporation equipped with a certain traditional and independent organisation, observing certain usages regarding food and marriage. Each group is free to pursue its own aims free from interference by others. The functions of the different castes were regarded as equally important to the well-being of the whole. The serenity of the teacher, the heroism of the warrior, the honesty of the business man, and the patience and energy of the worker all contribute to the social growth. Each has its own perfection.

The rules of caste bring about an adjustment of the different groups in society. The Brahmins were allowed freedom and leisure to develop the spiritual ideals and broadcast them. They were freed from the cares of existence, as gifts to them by others were encouraged and even enjoined. They are said to be above class interests and prejudices, and to possess a wide and impartial vision. They are not in bondage to the State, though they are consulted by the State. The State, as one of the groups in society, was essentially military in its organisation. Its specific function was to preserve peace and order, and see to it that the different groups worked in harmony and no confusion of functions arose. The Government was an executive organisation expected to carry out the best interests of the people. The Brahmins, as the advisors of the Government, point out the true interests of society.

The political and the economic life of the community is expected to derive its inspiration from the spiritual. This principle saved the State from becoming a mere military despotism. The sovereign power is not identified with the interests of the governing classes but with those of the people at large. While *dharma* represents the totality of the institutions by which the common weal is secured and the life of the people is carried on, Government is the political organisation which secures for all the conditions under which the best life can be developed. The State did not include the other institutions, trade guilds, family life, etc., which were allowed freedom to manage their own affairs. It did not interfere with art, science and religion, while it secured the external conditions of peace and liberty necessary for them all. Today, the functions of the State are practically unlimited, and embrace almost the whole of social life.

In spite of its attachment to the principle of non-violence, Hindu society made room for a group dedicated to the use of force, the Ksatriyas. As long as human nature is what it is, as long as society has not reached its highest level, we require the use of force. So long as society has individuals who are hostile to all order and peace, it has to develop controls to check the anti-social elements. These anti-social forces gather together for revolt when the structure of society is shaken by war or internal dissensions. It is a great tribute to the relative soundness of the social structure in Great Britain, in all its strata, that its industrial upheavals, such as the general strike of 1926, which continued for nine days, are marked by little criminality and rowdyism.

The economic group of the Vaisyas were required to suppress greed and realise the moral responsibilities of wealth. Property is looked upon as an instrument of service. In the great days of Hinduism, the possessor of property regarded it as a social trust and undertook the education, the medical relief, the water supply and the amusements of the community. Unfortunately at the present day in almost all parts of the world the strain of money-making has been so great that many people are breaking down under it. Love of wealth is disrupting social life and is tending to the suppression of the spiritual. Wealth has become means of self-indulgence, and universal greed is the cause of much of the meanness and cruelty which we find in the world. Hinduism has no sympathy with the view that 'to mix religion and business is to spoil two good things'. We ought not to banish spiritual values from life.

The unskilled workers and the peasants from the proletariat, the Sudras. These castes are the actual living members of the social body each centred in itself and working alongside one another in cooperation. When a new group is taken into the fold of Hinduism, it is affiliated with one of the four castes. Many of the races from outside were accepted as Ksatriyas. Mr. Jackson writes: "Those Indians indeed have a poor opinion of their country's greatness who do not realise how it has tamed and civilised the nomads of Central Asia, so that wild Turcoman tribes have been transformed into some of the most famous of the Rajput royal races".

The system of caste insists that the law of social life should not be cold and cruel competition, but harmony and cooperation. Society is not a field of rivalry among individuals. The castes are not allowed to compete with one another. A man born in a particular group is trained to its manner, and will find it extremely hard to adjust himself to a new way. Each man is said to have his own specific nature fitting him for his own specific function, and changes of *dharma* or function are not encouraged. A sudden change of function when the nature is against its proper fulfilment may simply destroy the individuality of the being. We may wish to change or modify our particular mode of being, but we have not the power to effect it. Nature cannot be hurried by our desires. The four castes represent men of thought, men of action, men of feeling, and others in whom none of these is highly developed. Of course, these are the dominant and not the exclusive characters, and there are all sorts of permutations and combinations of them which constitute adulterations and mixture. The author of the *Bhagavadgita* believes that the divisions of caste are in accordance with each man's character and aptitude. *Karma* is adapted to *guna*, and our qualities in nature can be altered only gradually. Since we cannot determine in each individual case what the aptitudes of the individuals are, heredity and training are used to fix the calling. Though the functions were regarded as hereditary, exceptions were freely allowed. We can learn even from lowly persons. All people possess all qualities though in different degrees. The Brahmin has in him the possibilities of a warrior. The *risis* of old were agriculturists and sometimes warriors too.

The caste idea of vocation as service, with its traditions and spiritual aims, never encouraged the notion of work as a degrading servitude to be done grudgingly and purely from the economic motive. The perfecting of its specific function is the spiritual aim which each vocational group set to itself. The worker has the fulfilment of his being through and in his work. According to the *Bhagavadgita*, one obtains perfection if one does one's duty in the proper spirit of non-attachment. The cant of the preacher who appeals to us for the deep-sea fishermen on the ground that they daily risk their lives, that other people may have fish for their breakfasts, ignores the effect of the work on the worker. They go to sea not for us and our breakfasts but for the satisfaction of their being. Our convenience is an accident of their labours. Happily the world is so arranged that each man's good turns out to be the good of others. The loss of artistic vitality has affected much of our industrial population. A building craftsman of the old days had fewer political rights, less pay and less comfort too, but he was more happy as he enjoyed his work. Our workers who enjoy votes will call him a slave simply because he did not go to the ballot-box. But his work was the expression of his life. The worker, whether a mason or a bricklayer, blacksmith or carpenter, was a member of a great cooperative group initiated into the secrets of his craft as an impressionable age. He was dominated by the impulse to create beauty. Specialisation has robbed the worker of pride in craft. Work has now become business, and the worker wants to escape from it and seeks his pleasure outside in cinemas and television. While the social aspirations of the working classes for a fuller life are quite legitimate, there is unfortunately an increasing tendency to interpret welfare in terms of wealth. The claims of materialism are more insistent in the present vision of social betterment. The improvement of human nature is the true goal of all endeavour, though this certainly requires an indispensable minimum of comfort to which the worker is entitled.

We are now face to face with class conflicts. There has grown up an intense class consciousness with elements of suspicion and hatred, envy and jealousy. We are no more content to bring up our children in our own manner of life, but are insisting that all doors must be opened to those equipped with knowledge. The difficulties are due to the fact that some occupations are economically more paying, and all wish to knock at the paying doors. Democracy is so interpreted as to justify not only the very legitimate aspiration to bring about a more equitable distribution of wealth, but also the increasing tendency for a levelling down of all talents. This is not possible. There will always be men of ability who lead and direct, and others who will obey and follow. Brains and character will come to the top, and within the framework of democracy we shall have an aristocracy of direction. It is not true that all men are born equal in every way, and everyone is equally fit to govern the country or till the ground. The functional diversities of workers cannot be suppressed. Every line of development is specific and exclusive. If we wish to pursue one we shall have to turn our attention away from others. While we should remove the oppressive restrictions, dispel the ignorance of the masses, increase their self-respect, and open to them opportunities of higher life, we should not be under the illusion that we can abolish the distinctions of the genius and the fool, the able organiser and the submissive worker. Modern democracies tend to make us all mere 'human beings', but such beings exist nowhere.

India has to face in the near future the perils of industrialism. In factory labour where men are mechanised, where they have little to do with the finished product and cannot take any pleasure in its production, work is mere labour, and it does not satisfy the soul. If such mechanical work cannot be done by machines, if men have to do it, the less of it they have to do the better for them. The more the work tends to become mechanical and monotonous, the more necessary it is that the worker should have larger leisure and a better equipment for the intelligent use of it. The standard of employment must be raised not merely in wages, but in welfare. Mechanical work should be economically more paying than even that of the artist or the statesman. For in the latter case work is its own reward. In ancient India the highest kind of work, that of preserving the treasures of spiritual knowledge, was the least paid. The Brahmin had no political power or material wealth. I think there is some justice in this arrangement, which shows greater sympathy for those whose work is soul-deadening. We have also to remember that the economic factor is not the most important in a man's life. A man's rank is not to be determined by his economic position. Gambling peers are not higher than honest artisans. The exaltation of the economic will lead to a steady degradation of character. Again, we should not forget that the individuals who constitute the nation cannot all pursue the one occupation of political leadership or military power, but will be disturbed into many employments, and these will tend to create distinctive habits and sympathies. Though there may be transfers from one group to another, they are not likely to be numerous.

We are not so certain today as we were a century ago that the individualistic conception of society is the last word in social theory. The moral advantages of the spiritual view of society as an organic whole are receiving greater attention. A living community is not a loose federation of competing groups of traders and teachers, bankers and lawyers, farmers and weavers, each competing against all the rest for higher wages and better conditions. If the members of the different groups are to realise their potentialities, they must share a certain community of feeling, a sense of belonging together for good or evil. There is much to be said from this point of view for the system of caste which adheres to the organic view of society and substitutes for the criterion of economic success and expediency a rule of life which is superior to the individual's interests and desires. Service of one's fellows is a religious obligation. To repudiate it is impiety.

Democracy is not the standardising of everyone so as to obliterate all peculiarity. We cannot put our souls in uniform. That would be dictatorship. Democracy requires the equal right of all to the development of such capacity for good as nature has endowed them with. If we believe that every type means something final, incarnating a unique possibility, to destroy a type will be to create a void in the scheme of the world. Democracy should promote all values created by the mind. Each kind of service is equally important for the whole. Society is a living organism, one in origin and purpose though manifold in its operations. There can be no real freedom in any section or class in a society so long as others are in bondage. It is a truly democratic ideal that is uttered in the words, "May all cross safely the difficult places of life, may all see the face of happiness, may all reach that right knowledge, may all rejoice everywhere". While the system of caste is not a democracy in the pursuit of wealth or happiness, it is a democracy so far as the spiritual values are concerned, for it recognises that every soul has in it something transcendent and incapable of gradations, and it places all beings on a common level regardless of distinctions of rank and status, and insists that every individual must be afforded the opportunity to manifest the unique in him. Economically we are a cooperative concern or brotherhood where we give according to our capacity and take according to our needs. Politically we enjoy equal rights in the sight of law, and these two enable us to attain true spiritual freedom. A just organisation of society will be based on spiritual liberty, political equality and economic fraternity.

In the social order we find that one dominant group invariably subordinates others. Under the feudal constitution of society the exercise of the military function was most esteemed. In modern capitalist organisations wealth dominates. In the Hindu scheme the cultural forms the highest and the economic lowest, for the cultural and the spiritual are ends in themselves and are not pursued for the sake of anything else. The highest in the social hierarchy is the true Brahmin, in whom we find a complete union of opposites, a self-sacrifice which is true freedom, a perfect self-control which is perfect service, absence of personal ambition along with the most intense devotion to the world. The valiant knight, the Ksatriya hero, is not the ideal of India, for he has not the vision of the whole. He identifies himself with one part as against another. He has always something opposed to him which he aims at overpowering. The Brahmin sage who sees the whole of life stands above parties and is centred in the whole surveying all manifestations. He would be untrue to himself if he identified himself with one part as against another. If he does not fight it is not because he rejects all fighting as futile, but because he has finished his fights. He has overcome all dissensions between himself and the world and is now at rest. Both Buddha and Christ were tempted by the Evil One, who had to be defeated before they could obtain freedom. *Maitri* or friendliness to all is the chief quality of the Brahmin and most of us cannot attain to it except by gradual steps. The good fighter is the preliminary to the wise sage. He who fights gallantly as a warrior gains practical insight through the battlefield and becomes mature for the divine peace of wisdom. Courage on the battlefield manifested in giving and receiving wounds, in dealing death and frankly meeting it, is praised by Aristotle and many militarists. The willingness to sacrifice one's life is the mark of the superior person. Courage becomes the chief virtue of the Ksatriya, but this type is not the highest, for Ksatriya valour, however sublimated, is the expression of the primitive in us. We shall have wars and soldiers so long as the brute in us is untamed. Even highly civilised men become brutal at times. The tendency to cruelty is repressed in them rather than outgrown.

In those awful moments of life when the soul stands facing a great wrong and is torn with anguish and indignation the Ksatriya exclaims: 'Now you shan't do that ; I'll kill you', and the true Brahmin will say, "Do not do that; I would rather die". The higher the man, the fewer are his rights and the more numerous his duties.

While the dreamer wishes to see his ideals realised immediately and entirely, the Hindu code insists on a gradual transformation. It takes note of the laws and conditions of reality. The misguided idealist is shocked by the imperfections of man, is exasperated by the slow progress achieved, attributes to all his own enthusiasm for ideals, dreams short cuts to the millennium, and thus joins the forces of revolt. The State tooks upon him as a danger to society. By protesting against the checks and controls he leaves society open to the assaults of anarchy. The wise plan is to keep our feet on earth and our eyes steady on the stars. Ideals have to be realised through the common clay of human nature, of which the high and the low, the wise and the foolish are made. If all men were wise, life would be a simple task; but as men are attempting to be wise with varying degrees of success, the problems of human life have the character they possess. The Hindu thinkers distinguish between the less evolved in whom the powers of self-analysis and self-direction have not arisen, and the more evolved or the twice-born who were graded into the three classes of Brahmin, Ksatriya and Vaisya. The different castes represent members at different stages of the road to self-realisation. However lowly a man may be, he can rouse himself sooner or later by the normal process of evolution to the highest level and obtain freedom from the vicissitudes of time. Room and time are found for each to take his natural level, and everyone who shows a tendency to rise is lifted to the level of his highest capacity.

Distinctions soon began to be made among the different occupations, and the privileges and restrictions caused the degradation of some groups. Whenever the hierarchical conception tended to endanger the spiritual status and equality of the different classes, protests were uttered. All irrational snobbery was denounced. An artisan is as much a civilised man as a warrior. In the early days of the human race, it is said, there were no class distinctions, since all are born from the Supreme. According to the *Sruti*, the fishermen, the slaves and the gamblers are all divine. The *Bhagavata* makes out that there is only one class even as there is only one God. Manu says that all men are born unregenerate by the first or physical birth, but become regenerate by the second or spiritual birth. Caste is a question of character. 'One becomes a Brahmin by his deeds not by his family or birth; even a *Candala* is a Brahmin if he is of pure character. Some of the great *risis* worshipped by the Brahmins are half-castes and hybrids. Vasistha was born of a prostitute, Vyasa of a fisherwoman, Parasara of a *Candala* girl. Condut counts and not birth. So for as the attainment of perfection is concerned, even the low castes can attain as much as the 'high'. Krishna says in *Bhagavadgita*, "Those who take refuge in me even of inferior birth, women and Sudras, they also attain the highest state. The outcastes who have devotion are entitled to get the saving knowledge through the name of God; women, Sudras and degraded Brahmins are entitled to get it through the *Tantras*." The passion for perfection burns with as keen a flame in the destitute as well as the opulent, the weak as well as the strong. Love is not the possession of a class; nor is imaginative piety a commodity to be brought in markets. Social distinctions disappear so far as these gifts go.

While we all are entitled to perfection, different people are allowed to use the methods which have come down to them through their own group forms. The three upper castes are entitled to obtain perfection through the performance of Vedic sacrifices which the fourth is not allowed to do. *Upanayana* or initiation ceremony and Vedic study were denied to them. Society was perhaps anxious to preserve its useful members from losing their heads over them. Saving knowledge can be gained apart from Vedic study and rights. Samkara allows that Sudras like *suta* and Vidura obtained the highest knowledge by virtue of their previous life. Through a study of the Epics and the *Puranas*, through meditation, fasting, and worship of God one can attain the Supreme. Every man from the simple fact of his manhood is capable of reaching perfection.

The struggle for equality has been with us from the beginning of India's history.

We have one evidence of it in the feud between Vasistha, the pillar of orthodoxy and the enemy of all innovation, and Visvamitra, the leader of the progressive and the champion of freedom and liberty. While the conservative Vasistha wanted the Vedic religion to be confined solely to the Aryans, Visvamitra tried to universalise it. The movement of the *Upanisads* was in spirit a democratic one. Buddhism, as is well known, undermines all hierarchical ideas. Samkara's philosophy was essentially democratic, and Ramanuja honoured members of the Sudra and the Pancama classes as Alvars.

The Vedic rule of life was confined to the people who developed under the stimulus of experience recorded in the *Vedas*. Its forms are singularly well marked in type, and those of others were sufficiently unlike them to justify a distinction. Each group was allowed to work out its life unfettered by alien ideas which might confuse or obliterate its aim. But soon these special forms were regarded as a sort of spiritual monopoly, and ideas of superiority and inferiority developed. The institution of caste came into being for the development of society, and the welfare of society today demands a breaking down of all suspicion of monopoly. With the general levelling up there will be a greater democratisation of the ideals. In the golden age only the Brahmins practised austerities, in the second both Brahmins and Ksatriyas, in the third the three upper classes, and in the fourth all the four classes. In other words, the Hindu scriptures should be thrown open at the present day to all people irrespective of their caste or sex.

To draw this brief exposition to an end, it may perhaps be useful to give a resume of the central spirit of Hinduism and its application to the problems of religion and society.

We see that the Hindu recognises one supreme spirit, though different names are given to it. In his social economy he has many castes, but one society. In the population there are many races and tribes, but all are bound together by one common spirit. Though many forms of marriage ore permitted, there is only one ideal aimed at. There is a unity of purpose underlying the multitudinous ramifications.

The world which is a perpetual flow is not all. Its subjection to law and tendency to perfection indicate that it is based on a spiritual reality which is not exhausted in any particular object or group of objects. God is in the world, though not as the world. His creative activity is not confined to the significant stages in the evolutionary process. He does not merey intervene to create life or consciousness, but is working continuously. There is no dualism of the natural and the supernatural. The spiritual is an emergent of the natural in which it is rooted. The Hindu spirit is that attitude towards life which regards the endless variety of the visible and the temporal world as sustained and supported by the invisible and eternal spirit.

Evil, error and ugliness are not ultimate. Evil has reference to the distance which good has to traverse. Ugliness is half-way to beauty. Error is a stage on the road to truth. They have all to be outgrown. No view is so utterly erroneous, no man is so absolutely evil as to deserve complete castigation. If one human soul fails to reach its divine destiny, to that extent the universe is a failure. As every soul is unlike all others in the world, the destruction of even the most wicked soul will create a void in God's scheme. There is no Hell, for that means there is a place where God is not, and there are sins which exceed his love. If the infinite love of God is not a myth, universal salvation is a certainty. But until it is achieved, we shall have error and imperfection. In a continuously evolving universe evil and error are inevitable, though they are gradually diminishing.

In religion, Hinduism takes its stand on a life of spirit, and affirms that the theological expressions of religious experience are bound to be varied. One metaphor succeeds another in the history of theology until God is felt as the central reality in the life of man and the world. Hinduism repudiates the belief resulting from a dualistic attitude that the plants in my garden are of God, while those in my neighbour's are weeds planted by the Devil which we should destroy at any cost. On the principle that the best is not the enemy of the good, Hinduism accepts all forms of belief and lifts them to a higher level. The cure for error is not the stake or the cudgel, not force or persecution, but the quiet diffusion of light.

In practical religion, Hinduism recognises that there are those who wish to see God face to face, others who delight in the endeavour to know the truth of it all. Some find peace in action, others in non-action. A comprehensive religion guides each along his path to the common goal, as all woo the same goddess though with different gifts. We must not give supreme and sole importance to our speciality. Perfection can be attained as a celibate, or a householder, or an anchorite. A rigid uniform outlook is wrong. The saintliness of the holy man does not render the steadfastness of the devoted wife or the simple innocence of the child superfluous. The perfection of every type is divine. "Whatsoever is glorious, good beautiful and mighty, understand that it goes forth from out of a fragment of my splendour".

The law of *Karma* tells us that the individual life is not a term, but a series. Fresh opportunities well be open to us until we reach the end of the journey. The historical forms we assume will depend on our work in the past. Heaven and Hell are higher and lower stages in one continuous movement. They are not external to the experiencing individuals. Purification is by means of purgation. The wages of sin is suffering. We need not regard sin as original and virtue as vicarious. We should do our duty in that state of life to which we happen to be called. Most of us have not a free hand in selecting our vocation. Freedom consists in making the best of what we have, our parentage, our physical nature and mental gifts. Every kind of capacity, every form of vocation, if rightly used, well lead us to the centre.

While the ideal of monogamy is held up as the best means for a complete mental and spiritual as well as physical understanding between husband and wife, other forms were permitted in view of the conditions of people with different ideals and interests, habits and desires. A happy marriage requires to be made by slow steps and with much patient effort. If incompatibility of temper is enough to justify divorce, many of us will be divorced. While woman's functions are distinguished from those of men, there is no suggestion of their inferiority.

While caste has resulted in much evil, there are some sound principles underlying it. Our attitude to those whom we are pleased to call primitive must be one of sympathy. The task of the civilised is to respect and foster the live impulses. of backward communities and not destroy them. Society is an organism of different grades, and human activities differ in kind and significance. But each of them is of value so long as it serves the common end. Every type has its own nature which should be followed. No one can be at the same time a perfect saint, a perfect artist, and a perfect philosopher. Every definite type is limited by boundaries which deprive it of other possibilities. The worker should realise his potentialities through his work, and should perform it in a spirit of service to the common weal. Work is craftsmanship and service. Our class conflicts are due to the fact that a warm giving sense of unity does not bind together the different groups.

These are some of the central principles of the Hindu faith. If Hinduism lives today, it is due to them, but it lives so little. Listlessness reigns now where life was once like a bubbling spring. We are today drifting, not advancing, waiting for the future to turn up. There is a lack of vitality, a spiritual flagging. Owing to our political vicissitudes, we ignored the law of growth. In the great days of Hindu civilisation it was quick with life, crossing the seas, planting colonies, teaching the world as well as learning from it. In sciences and arts, in trade and commerce it was not behind the most advanced nations of the world till the middle of this millennium. Today we seem to be afraid of ourselves, and are therefore clinging to the shell of our religion for self-preservation. The envelope by which we try to protect life checks its expansion. The bark which protects the interior of a tree must be as living as that which it contains. It must not stifle the tree's growth, but must expand in response to the inner compulsion. An institution appropriate and wholesome for one stage of human development becomes inadequate and even dangerous when another stage has been reached. The cry of conservatism 'it has always been thus' ignores the fundamentals of the theory of relativity in philosophy and practice, in taste and morals, in politics and society, of which the ancient Hindus had a clear grasp. The notion that in India time has stood still for uncounted centuries, and nought has been changed since the primeval sea dried up, is altogether wrong. While there has been continuity with the past, there has also been progress. The *Upanishads* are products of a perfectly spiritual movement which implicitly superseded the cruder ceremonial religion of the *Vedas*. When the movement of the *Upanisads* became lost in dogmatic controversies, when the fever if disputes and dialectics lulled the free spirit of religion, Buddhism called upon the people to adhere to the simplicity of truth and the majesty of the moral law. About the same period, when canonical culture and useless learning made religion inhuman scholasticism, and filled those learned in this difficult trifling with ridiculous pride, the *Bhagavadgita* opened the gates of heaven to all those who are pure in heart. When the ritualists succeeded in imprisoning the living faith in rigid creeds, the true prophets of the spirit, the *Saiva* and the *Vaisnava* saints, and the theologians like Samkara and Ramanuja, summoned the people to the worship of the living God. The influence of Madhva and Caitanya,

Basava and Ramananda, Kabir and Nanak is not inconsiderable. There has been no such thing as a uniform stationary unalterable Hinduism whether in point of belief or practice. Hinduism is a movement, not a position; a process, not a result; a growing tradition, not a fixed revelation. Its past history encourages us to believe that it will be found equal to any emergency that the future may throw up, whether in the field of thought or of history.

After a long winter of some centuries, we are today in one of the creative periods of Hinduism. We are beginning to look upon our ancient faith with fresh eyes. We feel that our society is in a condition of unstable equilibrium. There is much wood that is dead and diseased that has to be cleared away. Leaders of Hindu thought and practice are convinced that the times require, not a surrender of the basic principles of Hinduism, but a restatement of them with special reference to the needs of a more complex and mobile social order. Such an attempt will only be the repetition of a process which has occurred a number of times in the history of Hinduism. The work of readjustment is in process. Growth is slow when roots are deep. But those who light a little candle in the darkness will help to make the whole sky aflame.

6

ON POLITICS

Radhakrishnan was much closer to Gandhiji than to Nehru in his political thinking. Not that his Western liberal education had not left its mark on his thoughts. The important thing was that his politics was *Upanisadic*. But it was by no means backward looking. The birth of a new order out of the old was his recurring theme. He believed that the world, including humanity, though one in essence must become one in fact. He said, "If the old world has to die in violence, in catastrophe, in misery, terror and chaos, if it should fall bringing down with it much that is good, beautiful and true, spilling the blood, wasting the lives and warping the spirits of many, it is because we are unable peacefully to adjust ourselves to the new world, which all the time has been indivisible in essence and now is pressing to become indivisible in fact".[1] This view of the unity of all is most clearly expressed in his introduction to the Principal *Upanishads*. He said, "Essential unity with God is unity with one another through God. In the sense of heightened awareness we do not forget the world, which seems strangely of one piece. We are lifted out of provincialism into perspective, as we become aware of something vaster, profounder, more ultimate than the world".[2]

Radhakrishnan, though an ardent patriot, never allowed his patriotism to become anything like a narrow nationalism. He said, "Nationalism is not a 'national' instinct. It is an acquired artificial emotion. Love of one's native soil loyalty to regional traditions do not mean violent hostility to one's neighbours. If today the feeling of national pride is intense, it only shows the prodigious capacity of human nature for self-deception".[3] It was because of this deep Upanishadic faith that he was every inch a *visvamanava*, a universal human being.

Radhakrishnan takes pride in the fact that Hinduism is not bound up with a creed or a dogma, with a founder-prophet or a historical personality, with a book like the *Bible* or the *Quran*, but is a persistent search for truth on the basis of a continuously renewed experience. He, as an ardent Hindu, could not transcend Hinduism itself. He was respectful of all religions, but it is ultimately Hindu standards by which he judged other religions. Hinduism was always for him the ideal religion, of course, a Hinduism re-interpreted, purged of all that he found distasteful in it. For him, individual is all important. He said, "The strength of society is derived from that of forceful individuals. If individuality is lost, all is lost".[4] He attacked Christianity for its exaggerated other-worldliness, and for thereby separating religion and politics. But in his own thinking, he could not integrate the individual and society. He saw the relation between politics and religion primarily as an individual dialectic.

The relation between politics and religion was not primarily in institutions and movements for social change, but centred largely in the inner spiritual regeneration of the individual resulting in compassionate action in society. It would appear that, according to Radhakrishnan, spiritually insightful individuals would be the main transforming agents in society—not movements, institutions or organisations. He said, "Modern man without losing his social consciousness or conscience, must rediscover within himself a source of individual initiative sufficiently strong to cope with social despotisms".[5]

Mankind is a unit for Radhakrishnan, but religion itself is a primarily individual concern. This is partly an idea taken over from Western liberalism and often repeated today by members of our own secular elite. They say that politics is public while religion is private. For him, this Western liberal idea is confirmed by the Hindu tradition as it has developed. He recognises *dharma* as the principle of social integration in Hinduism.

Hindu *dharma* is based on the Hindu scriptures, including the *dharmasastras* or the example of *risis* and sages, and on a tradition that has come down to us from the ancient as well as the insights of conscience. But *dharma* is a living tradition. He said, "If we are wedded over-much to the rules of the past, if the living faith of the dead becomes the dead faith of the living, the civilisation will die".[6] He is strongly for change and renewal in the Hindu tradition itself. His view of the duty of regenerated or spiritual intellectuals, however, is not in terms of political action. He said, "The intellectuals need not take active part in politics or in the actual affairs of administration. It is their primary function to serve society with intellectual integrity. They must create the social consciousness and sense of responsibility which transcend the limits of political community. Those who can serve society in this way have a duty not to engage in politics. For every society there will be a few for whom participation in political activity would be a perversion of genius, a disloyalty to themselves".[7]

Radhakrishnan saw the need for sages staying out of party politics and out of striving for political power. Yet Gandhiji did identify himself with one political party and did engage in direct political action against British colonial power, against the partition of India, and against the oppression of the masses. Separation of politics and religion, which Radhakrishnan opposed, has proved to be practically impossible for India. It is not the separation of religion and politics that is remedy for our problems, it is the proper integration between a higher religious perspective and a politics devoted to the welfare of all. He suggested the spiritual development of individuals who without directly participating in political action, would still be able to transform the political economy by their example and inspiration. The wrong kind of religious sentiments are today exploited by politicians for personal and group benefit.[8]

Radhakrishnan contends that since life cannot be compartmentalised there can be no divorce between politics and religion either. He maintains that there is an important connection between politics and ethics and religion. For him, religion is the basis of society, hence the religious spirit of self-determination, tolerance, responsibility and love should permeate every sphere of life. He is aware that in actual fact political life is full of passion, prejudice, pride, self-interest, love of power, but it needs to be moralised for politics is a branch of ethics and is a means of promoting human welfare and happiness.

We should strive for an ideal society characterised by the reign of love. Radhakrishnan said, "Civilised society is possible only in an ordered community, where there is the rule of law".[9] The State and the entire political machinery exist in order to promote the individual's spiritual freedom and his creativity. He holds that the State requires to exercise coercion because of the imperfection of human nature which is visible in man's ambition, pride, lust, greed. He maintains that state power is not meant to enslave man. He is aware that power, whether exercised by individuals or by nations, is likely to be abused and it makes one arrogant and conceited. He maintains that power should be bridled by law, that the incorporation of fundamental rights in the Constitution, a strong vigilant public opinion and an active control of the religious conscience can safeguard the individual from the tyranny of government. He favours the state's use of force to curb human greed. He is not averse to the socialist policy of state ownership of public utilities and restrictions of forms of monopoly if the common weal requires it.[10]

To quote Radhakrishnan, "The state's existence is justified only if it promotes the sanctity, the dignity, the freedom and creativity of the human spirit".[11] So he suggests that government should provide financial assistance for the arts but it should not encroach on their autonomy. He thinks that Government stands to gain from free, honest, dispassionate constructive criticism provided by artists, thinkers engaged in solitary pursuits. To him, the promotion of justice, liberty and welfare are the functions of the state. He said, "The value of a society is to be measured, not so much by the sort of public order and efficiency it maintains, as by the degree to which its ways of action allow freedom of thought and expression, encourage moral decision and contribute to the development of the intelligence and good will of its members".[12]

Radhakrishnan thinks that democracy is a multi-faceted concept. Politically, it is self-government by means of adult franchise which seeks to secure the progress of all under the leadership of the wisest and the best. It is opposed to social and political totalitarianism. Democracy is government based on the people's consent, freedom and the rule of law. To him, power should be decentralised and the government's autocratic tendencies must be curbed. He thinks that economic backwardness, not caste or community, should be the criterion for special concessions. In a democracy, political freedom must be accompanied by economic justice. He thinks that the democratic technique of resolving issues by reason rather than by force makes for peace, non-disruptive and bloodless change, whether it be in the political realm or in the spheres of social and cultural rehabilitation. The democratic technique may be slow and cumbrous in its attempt to replace the politics of power by the politics of brotherhood. Democracy is an ethical temper. It involves the practice of self-restraint. It necessitates the individual's emancipation from pride, prejudice, greed, provincialism and non-compliance with corruption, nepotism.[13]

For Radhakrishnan, democracy is a scheme of life. He said, "It is a set of values and standards which expresses itself in every phase of living-personal, social, economic, political, international and inter-religious".[14] To him, the real unit of life is the individual and democracy is faith in man to govern and perfect himself and create a society conducive to this end. The democratic spirit is one of self-scrutiny, of *vinaya*, which is humility and discipline. He said, "Democracy as a way of life includes good faith, tolerance, respect for opinions which we do not share, equal justice for all, the power to speak one's own thoughts, to do one's duty as one sees it, to live under a government which he has a voice in making and unmaking, to promote the causes and advance the reforms which command his devotion, however repugnant they may be to the rulers".[15] He considers democracy to be the highest religion as it maintains the inviolability of the human personality by virtue of it being the concrete embodiment of the supreme. He opines that democracy is indivisible even though it is expressed in political, economic, social, cultural, ethical and religious terms.

Radhakrishnan opines that freedom is not the absence of all restraints but rather the substitution of rational ones for the irrational. He is not in favour of unbridled individualism but a socialised one where freedom of thought and action is permitted within limits of a reasonable social harmony. He opines that it is an important means to the good life. He holds that freedom is the right of self-determination. He said, "Freedom must not infringe upon the equal right of every other person or state to the same measure of self-determination".[16] He stresses that freedom has a spiritual quality by which it can break all barriers. He stresses that political freedom must be given a social economic content.

According to Radhakrishnan, socialism is not incompatible with democracy for it recognises human liberty. It does not signify an equalisation of all the abilities of individuals nor does it mean that all should be poor or starve equally. It is based on consent. It is ethical in character. He states that socialism is not a ruse to substitute state control for private enterprise. He does not rule out the possibility of the state running major concerns if it results in social uplift of the underprivileged. He makes it clear that socialism aims at equality of opportunity for all but not at a levelling of the abilities of individuals. He thinks that a welfare democratic socialist state should pursue economic security, intellectual life and spiritual freedom and promote unity among people of diverse creeds, races and regions. He stresses that state control should not lead to the loss of individual liberty.[17]

Radhakrishnan opines that everyone should be given opportunities for self-development irrespective of caste, race and religion. He makes it clear that in view of the differences between men which can never be wished away it is never possible for a social organisation to give absolute equality of opportunity and have equality of rewards. Injustice will result by treating equals unequally or by treating unequals equally. Deininger said, "Equality of opportunity treated as a need or a right, or as both, need not involve the view that men are entitled equally to succeed in what they undertake".[18] He regards equal distribution of wealth and opportunity to be an aim of democracy.

Radhakrishnan thinks that political freedom is meant to serve the ends of justice. The concept of justice is multi-dimensional. He defines social justice not as a scheme of rights but one of opportunities. He said, "No one should overlook intolerable, unjust and outrageous wrong and that justice must have power or else it is impotent, and power without it is tyranny".[19] Again, he said, "Political freedom and economic justice are two sides of democracy, which are both essential".[20]

One of the merits of democracy is that it makes social peace and stability. To Radhakrishnan, democracy is valuable, eventhough it may be inefficient and expensive. It guarantees civil and political liberties to its members. He thinks that parliamentary democracy is the best form of government. He opines that democracy is feasible in small states. He contends that it does not promote the rule of the best men. It is ruled by a mysterious caucus and elected representatives are tools of the machine of the state. Democracy has its limitations because voters are ignorant, unenlightened, unable to choose their leaders judiciously. He thinks that discontent with democracy also stems from the fact that it has not been able to tackle the problem of grave economic inequality, in the absence of which citizens can hardly be expected to take an active, honest part in public affairs. He holds that if democracy does not arrest the drift towards authoritarianism it will soon die.

Radhakrishnan states that Indian democracy is founded on the principles of national unity, secularism and peaceful social change. It aims at the production of a non-communal scientific welfare state. He thinks that Indian democracy is based on unity, in the sense that its teeming millions of people belonging to different races and creeds are bound together under simple administration, system of law, independent judiciary. He is aware that the adoption of democracy from Britain has all the difficulties attendant on grafting but later he remarks that the democratic spirit has entered the blood stream of India's history. He said, "In the administration of villages and towns caste and trade guilds, every individual is both sovereign and subject".[21]

Radhakrishnan thinks that the defects of Indian democracy are due to human frailty and the failure of social institutions. He believes that a society founded on poverty and exploitation is an immoral one and is eventually bound to collapse, for it like a house built on shifting sands. He states that a society that tolerates the scourge of untouchability has no right to call it self civilised. He observes that the clash between caste and out-caste is growing more intense and bitter, that it is both a political and administrative evil since the priestly classes still occupy the dominant positions in social life. He thinks that the British influence has been both degrading and beneficial. He said, "Britain ruled India by resort to special powers, by imprisoning representatives even while proclaiming the right of self-government".[22] He states that the British provided India with railways, irrigation works, law and an efficient administration. He thinks that we owe a great debt of gratitude to Britain for making us conscious of our destiny as a nation, for making us aware of the responsibility of government, for her spirit of exploration and inquiry, which has provided us the opportunity to study not only our own cultural heritage, but also those of other lands.[23]

The quality of a democracy depends ultimately on the character of the men who comprise it. Radhakrishnan stresses that the prime requirement of a spiritually sick society is that we must be reborn in the spirit. He said, "We must discover roots in the eternal, regain faith in transcendent truth which will order life, discipline the discordant elements and bring unity and purpose in it".[24] He thinks that education is a potent means to bring about a spiritual regeneration and social emancipation of the people. He stresses that education is valuable only if it is given a spiritual direction, or else it well make men demonic, intellectually conceited, spiritually crass and cold hearted. The true democrat does not hold office for his personal ambition. He has both qualities of mind and heart. Public opinion, more than one party system, a free and responsible press, decentralisation and hard work are the other factors that make democracy successful. He is not in favour of a single party in a democracy. All parties should abide by constitutional objectives. The press should be responsible and serve as an instrument of education, of public opinion by reporting dispassionately and intelligently and being guided by the principles of our Constitution. He suggests that Indian democracy should take to decentralisation by means of the *Panchayat Raj*.

Radhakrishnan maintains that dictatorship is not conducive to man's nature and development. It stifles man's freedom and thus retards growth. It tolerates no dissent. It demoralises and dehumanises those in power so that they become corrupt, greedy for self and power.

Communism arose as a protest against the despicable conditions of the working class with the advent of the Industrial Revolution. Radhakrishnan said, "Communist social philosophy is to be distinguished from the technique of government with communist countries adopt which is one of coercion and violence".[25] So he opines that the totalitarian character of modern communism is illiberal, unrighteous and even un-Marxist. He thinks that Marxism is a spirit, not a programme, a method of social analysis, not an interpretation of texts. He maintains that Marx is incorrect in regarding the economic factor as the sole determinant of history. He thinks that if society advances due to the play of materialist forces, there is no reason why the new egalitarian society established by the workers will be exempt from the law of dialectical progress. He does not agree with the original Marxian view and that of the communists who think that socialist goals can be realised through violent techniques. He is not opposed to private property. He thinks that many poverty-stricken people are attracted to communism because it gives them hope for a better life, by its rational allocation of resources and opportunities, which brings about a more equitable distribution of wealth.[26]

Radhakrishnan is also aware of the limitations of communism. He thinks that initially communism aimed at efficiency at the cost of individual freedom, sought to regiment the life of the individual, stifled creativity in art, religion, science and philosophy and offered equal rewards for all types of work, which resulted in a slackening of effort, promoted dictatorship and did not attain its goal of a classless society. He maintains that communism is more sober and willing to defend democracy so it should not be identified with violence, irreligion, tyranny and individual suppression. He explains that concentration camps have given way to labour correction camps. He thinks that as collective leadership increases there is more scope for democratic control of state policies. To him, communism is only against dogma-based religion which supports inequalities and vested interests; it is not against religion which aims at personal integration, and a just and equitable social order. He admits that neither democracy nor communism are flawless. He thinks that democracy has deteriorated because it has tried to control man whereas communism is moving relentlessly towards an open society. He said, "Democracy and communism suffer from faith in the omnipotence of mechanism and technique and the spirit of materialism".[27]

Radhakrishnan views nationality as a corporate and spiritual sentiment. He also maintains that there is nothing ultimate, definite or fixed about a nation. To him, nationalism signifies the resolve that the people of a country will do their utmost to preserve its soul, its integrity, and contribute to the progress of the world community. He said, "Nationalism is the consciousness which nations have acquired of their genius when once they are personified."[28] Genuine nationalism is consistent with internationalism. He thinks that nation states arose when men felt the need for a central power to call a halt to feuds and civil wars. To him, a nation is great not by its size or wealth but by the pains it takes to enlarge its spirit, to build men of character who will work selflessly, dedicatedly and detatchedly to remove the disabilities of their compatriots. He is all too aware of the disastrous consequences of aggressive nationalism, which lapses into imperialism. He opines that the pursuit of unbridled nationalism has resulted in mass egotism, self-idolatry, reduction of the world into a babel of people and has proved to be an obstacle to cooperation and friendship. He said, "Successive waves of internationalism broke on the shores of local pride and national unity".[29]

To quote Radhakrishnan, "India is a nation for it is not a geographical expression, nor is it a collection of individuals, it is tradition, an order of thought and manners, a loyalty to certain fundamental values fostered by all races and religions that have found a home in this land".[30] He believes that India has always sought to promote the cult of the spirit and has never pursued the path of national aggrandizement. He thinks that India has always been the standard bearer of culture as a large part of the world received its religious education from India. He maintains that Indian culture is a composite and variegated fabric, a rich amalgam of Aryan, Dravidian, Hindu, Buddhist, Muslim, British and other Western influences. He points out that for centuries our country has been referred to as a unity as testified by the Chinese travellers and the accounts given in the epics, and classics, which have been corroborated by others.

National unity can be fostered by sinking differences arising from racial, religious and casteist differences and by doing away with the obnoxious aspects of our past. Radhakrishnan said, "National unity should be deliberately and carefully nurtured for if we lose our sense of belonging to one nation, we will lose our identity and our capacity to control our future will be diminished if not destroyed".[31] He believes that war has a therapeutic effect on a faction ridden people who are then roused to preserve their freedom and territorial integrity. He thinks that education is a powerful agency to break down barriers between men and to enable to work for common goals. He pleads for the retention of English and two or more official languages. He advocates that irrespective of caste, community or creed, the economically backward be given opportunities for selfreliance. He thinks that Indians must not despair but face obstacles with honesty and seriousness. Nationalism is not incompatible with internationalism but is a step that leads to it.

Internationalism signifies that every independent nation strives to realise its potentialities whilst recognising its links, obligations and union with other nations, Radhakrishnan considers national autonomy as a pre-condition to world fellowship. He contends that the unity of the world is being shaped by logic of events. He thinks that distinctions among men on the basis of race, religion, nationality are of no consequence and the only important difference is whether they are civilised or not. He points out that whilst science and technology have brought about a physical unification it is up to man to world for intellectual communication and spiritual communion. He thinks that man must realise that neither material wealth nor political power can thrive without moral foundations. He contends that nationalism paves the way for internationalism. International law must be adopted at the international level to promote internationalism. Factors like clean administration, devoted leadership, economic opportunities, national cohesion, common ideals and aspiration, would be conducive in promoting the cause of nationalism. He thinks that the present brand of aggressive nationalism has to make way for loyalty to humanity. National sovereignty should prevail in domestic and economic matters. He maintains that negotiation, adjustment methods will not work if we adopt a shopkeeper's attitude. To him, compromise does not stand for laxity in morals but a peaceful way of making adjustments. He is of the opinion that amity and fraternity of mankind can be promoted if men get together not just in the political fields but also in other areas. He welcomes East-West dialogue and ventures to solve global problems and meet challenges.[32] He thinks that harmony can be fostered if men are acquainted with the life and teachings of great universalists. Religious idealism is the most potent instrument for peace, fellowship and cooperation. He said, "Internationalism requires patience, perspective and understanding. It requires us to meet abuse by courtesy, obstruction by reasonableness. Suspicion and hatred by trust and goodwill".[33]

Radhakrishnan thinks that UN serves as a meeting ground between different factors in the world. It ensures cooperation on issues where there is agreement and it provides a platform for debate on controversial problems. He is aware of several factors that impede the working of the UNO, which he considers to be the nearest approximation to world government. He envisages that the international authority alone should have the power to declare war. To him, the original *Panchshila* enunciated by Buddha centred round the principles of restraint, of truth speaking, of reverence for life and respect for fellowmen, of freedom from avarice and abstinence from intoxicating drinks. He clarifies that non-alignment does not mean neutrality towards right, nor does it mean isolationism nor does it signify an attitude of superiority, which divides the world into two fixed groups.

Radhakrishnan thinks that war is a climax of misunderstanding, though at times it is undertaken to seek justice. It is an acquired mental habit wherein man alone, decides to kill for metaphysical reasons. He regards cold war to be a state of armed fear. He considers war to be an outrage on all that is human since it plunges millions into death, starves children, defiles women. It is a renewal of barbarism and reveals man's spiritual blindless. He said, "War arises because of man's selfishness, greed, thirst for power, worship of politics, because he has dispensed with obedience, humility and above all because of obsessive fear which is even worse than hate".[34] He thinks that wars are also fought to secure justice and peace, preserve democracy, protect women and homeland, fight racial injustice. He maintains that a state when attacked has the bounden duty to protect its citizens and that a just war is liberative and non-aggressive. He thinks that the use of force is justified at both national and international levels to maintain order, restrain the evil doer, protect the helpless, uphold the rule of law. He favours the resolution of conflict not by coercion but by negotiation, arbitration and adjustment.

Radhakrishnan opines that the unilateral cessation of nuclear tests is a step towards complete disarmament. Though he regards peace as tolerance or mutual forbearance, he does not conceive it to be just a negative state of absence of strife and conflict nor is it that which can be attained by bluffing, bargaining and bullying. He is aware that making peace pacts, granting independence to nations, will not automatically ensure peace. Peace signifies faith in the invisible spirit of man and is meant to be not just an intellectual achievement but a moral and spiritual one. He is emphatic that self-security and international discipline on the part of sovereign states are important. He said, "If men conquer their own inordinate desires, this inner victory will show forth in their outer relations".[35] It is man's conscious and continuous effort that can make the world safe for peace.

REFERENCES

1. Radhakrishnan, S., *Religion and Society*, p. 19.
2. Radhakrishnan, S., *The Principal Upanisads*, p. 87.
3. Radhakrishnan, S., *Religion and Society*, p. 14.
4. *Ibid.*, p. 77.
5. *Ibid.*
6. *Ibid.*, p. 117.
7. *Ibid.*, p. 228.
8. Parthasarathi, G., *Radhakrishnan Centenary Volume*, p. 310.
9. Radhakrishnan, S., *Education, Politics and War*, p. 83.
10. Rodrigues, C., *The Social and Political Thought of Dr. S. Radhakrishnan*, pp. 162-163.
11. Radhakrishnan, S., *Religion and Society*, pp. 60-61.
12. Ibid., p. 64.
13. Rodrigues, C., *op. cit.* pp. 164-165.
14. Radhakrishnan, S., *Report of the University Education Commission*, Vol. I, p. 63.
15. Radhakrishnan, S., *The Present Crisis of Faith*, p. 43.
16. Radhakrishnan, S., *Religion and Society*, p. 66.
17. Rodrigues, C., *op. cit.*, pp. 167-168.
18. Deininger, W.T., *Problems in Social and Political Thought*, p. 262.
19. Radhakrishnan, S., *Occasional Speeches and Writings*, p. 207.
20. *Ibid.*, p. 135.
21. Radhakrishnan, S., *Eastern Religions and Western Thought*, p. 370.
22. Ray, S.K., *The Political Thought of Radhakrishnan*, p. 45.
23. Rodrigues, C., *op. cit.*, pp. 173-175.
24. Ray, S.K., *op. cit.*, p. 45.
25. Radhakrishnan, S., *Recovery of Faith*, p. 58.
26. Rodrigues, C., *op. cit.*, pp. 177-179.
27. Radhakrishnan, S., *East and West—Some Reflections*, p. 115.
28. Radhakrishnan, S., *Occasional Speeches and Writings*, p. 69.
29. Radhakrishnan, S., *Religion and Culture*, p. 75.
30. Radhakrishnan, S., *Education, Politics and War*, p. 197.
31. Radhakrishnan, S., *Occasional Speeches and Writings*, p. 275.
32. Rodrigues, C., *op. cit.*, pp. 185-188.
33. Radhakrishnan, S., *Occasional Speeches and Writings*, p. 8.
34. *Ibid.*, p. 211.
35. Radhakrishnan, S., *Eastern Religions and Western Thought*, p. 384.

BIBLIOGRAPHY

Books by Radhakrishnan

The Hindu View of Life
The Religion We Need
An Idealist View of Life
East and West in Religion
Education, Politics and War
Religion and Society
The Bhagavad Gita
Indian Philosophy, Volume one
Recovery of Faith
East and West
The Brahma Sutra
Occasional Speeches and Writings
Religion in a Changing World
Freedom and Culture
True Knowledge
Philosophy of Life Values
Eastern Religion and Western Thought

Books on Radhakrishnan

Gopal, S., *Radhakrishnan: A Biography.*
Joad, C.E.M., *Counter Attack from the East: The Philosophy of Radhakrishnan.*
Naravane, V.S., *Modern Indian Thought.*
Parthasarathi, G., and Chattopadhyaya, D.P., *Radhakrishnan Centenary Volume.*
Raj, S.K., *The Political Thought of President Radhakrishnan.*
Rodrigues, C., *The Social and Political Thought of Dr. S. Radhakrishnan.*
Shrimali, K.L., *A Search for Values in Indian Education.*
Singhal, D.P., *Modern Indian Society and Culture.*

INDEX